BIASES AND DANGERS *in* ARTIFICIAL INTELLIGENCE

Developing Global Policy for Safe and Beneficial Use of Artificial Intelligence

ELLEN D. CRAYTON, MBA

DISCLAIMER

The information presented in this book solely and fully represents the views of the author as of the date of publication. Any omission, or potential misrepresentation of any peoples or companies, is entirely unintentional. As a result of changing information, conditions or contexts, this author reserves the right to alter content at their sole discretion with impunity.

This book is for informational and entertainment purposes only and while every attempt has been made to verify the information contained herein, the author assumes no responsibility for errors, inaccuracies, and omissions. Each person has unique needs and this book cannot take these individual differences into account. For ease of use, all links in this book are redirected through this link to facilitate any future changes and minimize dead links.

Copyright © 2019 "**ELLEN D. CRAYTON**" all rights reserved. It is illegal to copy, distribute, or create derivative works from this book in whole or in part. No part of this book may be reproduced or transmitted in any form whatsoever, electronic, or mechanical, including photocopying, recording, or by any informational storage or retrieval system without expressed written, date and signed permission from the author.

I dedicate this book to Olivia Ellen Stakhursky, my beautiful granddaughter, born on Friday, January 8, 2021, who encouraged me to complete the book.

Table of Content

Introduction 1

Chapter 1 – What Is AI Policy And Why Do We Need It? 3

Chapter 2 – Influences In AI Diffusion 7

Chapter 3 – Policies And Consequences 27

Chapter 4 – Possible AI Policies' Classification 31

Chapter 5 – Legal, Ethical, And Other Challenges 39

Chapter 6 – Malevolent Control Of AI Technology 47

Chapter 7 – The Liability Allocation Question 55

Chapter 8 – Equitable Distribution 61

Chapter 9 – Counterintelligence 65

Chapter 10 – Ethics In Machine Learning 91

Chapter 11 – Why Regulating AI Could Be Difficult 95

Chapter 12 – AI Technologies And Their Use Cases 101

Chapter 13 – Making The Case For Policy 123

Chapter 14 – Overriding Policy Formulation Principle 133

Chapter 15 – Policy Formulation For AI Control 139

Chapter 16 – Guiding Principles and Recommendations 143

Chapter 17 – The Key Aspects of AI Policy 151

Conclusion 155

Sources and References 165

INTRODUCTION

Artificial Intelligence is everywhere. Artificial intelligence has the potential to bring about a paradigm shift and develop a significant impact on the digital economy and society. Information systems with ever more intelligence are already penetrating numerous areas of work and life.

A combination of rapidly increasing computing power, big data, and optimized algorithms have led to the current wave of progress and popularity for AI. What seemed unrealistic just a few years ago is a reality today. In the context of digitalization and a data-driven economy, the range of uses for AI systems will expand even further, from supporting human activities with intelligent cognitive systems, robots that can interact safely and adaptively with humans, intelligent and autonomous devices on the Internet of Things to self-driving vehicles that could be on our roads in just a few years.

People, companies, and governments are grappling with the best way to harness its massive potential for business gain and a better human experience in the coming decades. Already, the technologies have been used to change how you do politics, drive around, access medical care, trade, and even wage war. In short, AI will bring about the most significant disruption that you have ever seen; both good and bad.

As global efforts must be urgently geared towards the implementation of appropriate policies to define the boundaries with which AI can be developed this book examines the aspects, influences, and requirements that derive from the urgent need to govern AI and its diffusion. In particular, the Author seeks to provide a simple yet pragmatic approach to AI, its upsides and uses, and challenges, dangers, and pitfalls. In doing so, this publication arises under consideration of current concerns a variety of crucial questions to further discussion and provide food for thought.

CHAPTER 1

WHAT IS AI POLICY AND WHY DO WE NEED IT?

The rapid development and use of Artificial Intelligence (AI) have, without a doubt, created significant economic and societal interests. Individuals marvel at a device's ability to unlock their smartphones through face ID only to read personalized social media and news feeds. Businesses actively adopt AI to reduce costs, improve efficiency, detect and prevent fraud, and develop predictive purchasing analytics and algorithms. Inevitably, the notion that AI technologies will bring economic changes through productivity increases is no longer prognostication. But poses a challenge as to how the benefits are distributed without creating different outcomes for labor markets and society as a whole.

In this sense, one must question the potential effect of automation beyond the aspects of greater efficiency and cheaper consumer products. And in doing so, turn one eye to the likely replacement of unskilled and low-paying jobs and one to the consequential higher demand for a few highly skilled jobs. This, in turn, will likely result in a degree of structural unemployment, with the accompanying pitfall of making it harder to match jobs available to the demanded skill levels. This means that the global economy could find itself persistently battling high natural unemployment rates and eventually collapse under an AI-induced recession.

In addition, a second observation derives from the subsequent division of labor, which on a global scale will reset the status quo. Thus, shifting economic power away from long-established global players and towards emerging players that can naturally satisfy the need for cognitive labor at lower costs. And as a result, propel specific countries into economic superpowers whilst forcing greater inequality between those societies that cannot as easily supply the required workforce. This will cause inequality and naturally lead to technological distrust and anti-competitive practices. AI might then be blamed for causing global disruption.

Against this background, it becomes clear that the widespread use of AI mandates regulators and governments to ensure that the utilization of intelligent technologies remains rational and controllable. However, when considering that the development of AI and a move towards ASI not only to a great extent creates an overlap between capable societies. It requires undivided efforts and a well-concerted regime of global leadership. Therefore, the common objective of uniformly governed AI can only be based on a "run with the pack" approach that aims to strike a balance between minimizing risks and maximizing benefits.

This objective reveals the rather complex requirement of maintaining oversight in a constantly and rapidly evolving field while putting pressure on any single government to make the first step in delivering a deliberate system of principles, procedures, and protocols. However, satisfying the balancing act cannot be accomplished by simply setting initial regulatory safeguards as to an individual's rights and personal freedoms. Unavoidably, it requires the private sector and, in particular, technology giants to make the first step and formulate best practices.

This, in turn, may encourage a single lawmaker to produce a policy that holds the ability to be adaptable across the globe without compromising rigid legal concepts and proactively engaging in current and new development. The earlier mentioned objective indisputably broadens further and illustrates that AI strategy becomes a crucial factor when planning to develop policy.

However, as AI remains, due to the capability of rapid development, incredibly difficult to predict, it may simply not be enough to advance an overarching strategy that addresses geopolitical instability related to human-level or ASI. But, instead, to focus on a short-term AI strategy that governs concurrent challenges, including those deriving from driverless cars, small-scale worker displacement, algorithmic bias, and increasingly automated surveillance.

And, of course, the long-term effect must also be addressed. It will become necessary to persistently refine policy, including areas such as investments in skill development, workforce modernization, the creation of new regulations and standards, and targeted efforts to remove bias from AI algorithms and data sets. Yet the question is to what extent can such be turned into a long-term strategy when considering the unpredictability of AI development remains unanswered but aids in identifying a shared responsibility for AI policy between both society and lawmakers.

Therefore, it can be summarized that the current diffusion of AI into our daily lives not only brings on a vast selection of benefits; it also has the capability of posing significant threats to labor markets and society. In particular, when neglecting to control AI in its early stages, it is entirely possible to further global inequality and cause severe disruptions deriving from AI's potential to develop rapidly. Having to face the consequences, including an AI-induced recession, technological distrust, and anti-competitive practices will naturally contradict the benefits created from AI. It becomes clear that AI governance at early stages gains a level of significance that is parallel to AI development.

Nonetheless, efforts to regulate AI require uniformity and unanimous agreement in all policy areas to maintain the balance between minimizing risks and maximizing benefits. However, as lawmakers are unlikely to succeed in making the first step, it becomes evident that controlling AI diffusion must begin with the private sector to formulate best practices. Over time this could lead to a successful AI diffusion strategy and eventually produce global AI policies that consistently address both the short and long-term aspects of developing AI.

CHAPTER 2
INFLUENCES IN AI DIFFUSION

As diffusing AI essentially relies on the premise of mimicking human abilities to perform human tasks, Machine learning (ML), a subset of AI, is used to train machines how to learn. While most of us are familiar with the practical application of ML from Friday night movie recommendations or purchase suggestions. The basic process behind ML can be summarized as to supply data to an algorithm, from which the algorithm then generates rules based on the data supplied and then to advance and/or to develop a new algorithm.

Personal information

Gathering data, including personal information, has become the driving force of the internet and has led to an abundance of data available to learning algorithms and, thus, theoretically offers an ideal playing field for AI development. The recent advancement in data protection law seems to directly contradict artificial intelligence.

It is here that, for example, the EU's General Data Protection Regulation (GDPR) stipulates data minimization, the prohibition of automated decision making, and is topped with setting a strict transparency requirement. This mandates that only the data needed to achieve a particular purpose must be processed without automation and in a way that is easily explained to data subjects. Europe seems to have taken a stance against self-learning algorithms as those are often exceedingly complex, and the genesis of their results is not always understandable even to experts. Yet, on closer examination of the GDPR, elevating the preceding paragraph into a firm conclusion would be erroneous. Simply because the conflicts can be resolved when anonymizing collected data and then processing it in an anonymized fashion and thus ensuring that no reference to personal information is left and that the data subject is not identifiable.

Consequently, one may argue that if AI uses only anonymous data, the data protection law is not applicable. However, this raises the question of defining how personal data is anonymized and, as such, depends primarily on the efforts made to do so. When further considering that artificial intelligence can easily be used to reinstate data records that were previously considered anonymous with the help of the technology, a significant privacy concern arises.

In addition, tension is created if AI's self-learning capabilities grow beyond the point of being comprehensible to its developers. Known as the black box AI phenomenon, a lack of control subsequently creates an impenetrable system where the algorithm takes millions of data points as inputs and correlates specific data features to produce an output based on its own decisions. As this would simply deprive companies, organizations, and lawmakers of the ability to view, understand, and reconcile, errors, including unlawful processing of personal information, will go unnoticed until the effect becomes so significant that it is necessary to investigate and the damage caused may be expensive or even impossible to remedy.

As this would not only challenge the purpose of data protection and citizens' rights to security of their data but jeopardize rules of fair data practices and competition. The only recourse may then be a more aggressive legislative response to reinstate balance. However, as too much privacy regulation would hinder companies in the development and too little privacy protection will certainty discourage data subjects from participating in innovation and market transactions the objective turns into a conundrum. Yet when recalling that existing empirical work does not focus specifically on AI, but uses rather general and somehow ambiguous terms one can argue that current legislation hints the existence of a potential trade-off between the right to privacy and the speed of innovation. Which in turn signifies that any government strategy focused on AI must weigh the potentially conflicting interests of data processors and data subjects.

AI Bias

Another important aspect is likely to be the issue of discrimination. It is often assumed that bias occurs intentionally or by an oversight on the part of engineers or programmers. At the same time, not all biases need to be considered deliberate. For example, when an algorithm precisely achieved the goal that it was given or when the systems are trained with the help of data gathered from the Internet, and the biases present have been involuntarily adopted. Thus, AI bias can be introduced due to conscious or unconscious prejudices on the part of the developers or can creep into an algorithm through undetected errors.

When further exploring the matter of bias, one can identify preexisting bias. In terms of AI, this type of bias is established in society and transferred into the algorithm. As mentioned briefly above, this can happen explicitly if a discriminatory attitude is deliberately built-in or implicitly, if it is known from the field of predictive policing. For example, the biases of police officers are reflected in the locations and case numbers investigated or if historical job applications are used to train AI systems in the processing of new applications.

In addition, a technical bias occurs, for example, in sensor technology where an automatic soap dispenser was set up and tested without regard to various types of skin colors and did not respond to others. Another example would be standards that do not allow certain properties to be captured where information is translated from human terms into mathematical models. An illustration of this can be found when looking at search engine results. It is here that the results on the first page of a search engine are more likely to be clicked than the results on the following pages. However, as the search results are displayed on the first page depending on the screen size, it becomes clear that certain groups of people or specific data are treated differently than others.

A further type of bias can be identified as emergent bias. In such instances, discrimination arises from the interaction of software and application. In particular, the misinterpretation of outputs, which often occurs when using statistical values. Similarly, in circumstances where software developed for a specific purpose is used in a different context. For example, where social patterns of action, values, or processes change, and the algorithm has not been adjusted or does not automatically adapt to it.

Therefore, discrimination can arise from implicitly or explicitly biased inputs or technical decisions in the design. This can be called discriminatory input, and in principle, it can be identified by analyzing the system and the input data. However, in practice, the size and complexity of the data sets and source code would render any correction extremely challenging, if not impossible.

In contrast, some forms of discrimination only arise from its application and can only be detected in the algorithm's operation or test runs of the relevant output. A prime example can be found in the test version of the chat robot "Tay," which caused controversy when the bot began to post inflammatory and offensive tweets through its Twitter account. This was due to "Tay" being deliberately "fed" with xenophobic and discriminatory conversations by organized users and consequently "learned" to use inappropriate language.

At this point, a further challenge is implied. It can be summarized when suggesting that much of the discriminatory output of an algorithm will not be determinable before the event and may not even always be traceable after the event. This is likely to present a further challenge when considering that different forms of bias and discrimination can occur in different combinations.

While a legal system based on the principle of human dignity and human rights could provide a reliable foundation for developing and applying learning systems that do not discriminate against individuals or groups, it must be clarified at the societal level that artificial intelligence is not per se more neutral or more objective than humans and thus eliminates existing discrimination. Therefore, it becomes significant to policy to raise awareness of the discrimination risks that may be associated with the use of learning systems.

However, as one may argue, the existence of technical approaches that attempt to integrate ethical principles into the algorithm's design process, including Value Sensing, Value Sensitive Design, or Constructive Technology Assessment, will be a milestone when developing AI. It must be understood that the technical approach alone is insufficient since the social embeddedness of the algorithms not only relies on the areas of application but the development processes and the surrounding socio-political policies.

Further, those must include mechanisms that enable people without in-depth specialist knowledge to avoid dependencies on decisions made by algorithms and to be able to question and assess machine-made decisions. For example, through appropriate education and awareness-raising initiatives, producing an appropriate policy that efficiently addresses the concerns raised from AI bias may well require AI to provide a first draft.

Zero Trust

The classic perimeter security approach is no longer the best option for enterprise IT departments in today's environments. A far more flexible approach is needed, focusing on users, devices, and services. The Zero Trust concept was developed to counter current and future security threats. It is based on the premise that no person, device, or service inside or outside the enterprise network should be trusted.

Implementing the principles of the Zero Trust approach allows organizations to take full advantage of the security model. But in fact, this process is never truly complete; it is a constant evolution. Starting with the initial implementation, a constant re-examination that goes through each principle is necessary and continues until the process starts again, only to find that one's zero-trust model must constantly evolve to reflect changes in business processes, goals, technologies, and threats. Moreover, it is crucial to map and understand the entire attack surface, all users, devices, data, and services, including the means of transport through which sensitive corporate data passes must be included. Thus, Zero Trust Security naturally lends itself to the use of ML and the deployment of ever-increasing self-learning algorithms.

Once it is clear what needs to be protected, the next step is evaluating existing tools, combined with insights into the areas to be protected. It is important to identify where existing tools need to be deployed or re-positioned to reach the extended domains, such as cloud resources. In many cases, existing tools will not satisfy a complete, end-to-end zero-trust approach, and additional tools must be added to introduce more layers of protection when security gaps are identified in the zero-trust implementation. In addition, advanced threat protection tools can be used to identify new threats, which allows security policies to be placed exactly where they are needed for protection.

After all the necessary elements and technologies are in place to build a zero-trust framework, security admins must combine and deploy the tools accordingly. This is achieved by consistently creating and implementing zero-trust policies, which can then be applied to the various security tools. As soon as these very granular policies are created, administrators can configure security tools and devices to adhere to these rules while denying everything else.

The last important principle of a zero-trust model is implementing the necessary monitoring and the use of appropriate alerts. These tools provide security managers with an adequate overview of whether the implemented policies are working as planned or whether gaps are being exploited in the implemented system. The preceding and admittedly very brief explanation of distributed security architecture shows that Zero Trust Security can be a huge challenge to monitor properly. Certainly, modern monitoring tools with AI capabilities and automation features will eventually usurp the need for professionals to monitor networks and to detect and respond while simultaneously identifying root causes and taking corrective action.

Further and when drawing from the above illustration, one can identify that machine learning is revolutionizing Zero Trust Security Concepts in three ways, namely the adaptation to risk, policy alignment, and advanced contextual intelligence. When recalling the above-mentioned challenges when corresponding to risk, it is only obvious that many businesses have realized that a risk-driven approach prevails over a compliance-driven approach. As such, machine learning becomes responsible for assessing user, device, and behavioral data while simultaneously determining the real-time risk score for each access request. However, this process increases in complexity with every single access request as quantifying each risk score requires considering multiple factors, including the location of the access attempt, browser type, operating system, endpoint device status, user attributes, time of day, and unusual recent privilege change. Further, since each access also needs to be monitored according to the user's behavior and, for example, take into account unusual access histories, and privileges requested, etc., the adaptation to risk simply becomes impossible to manage effectively without the use of ML.

When continuing on the matter, the subject of policy alignment becomes the pivot in Zero Trust Strategy. It is here that analyzing and responding to users' behavioral patterns has turned in an effective way to scale and develop a business. While website traffic and monitoring tools provide an entry-level solution for those seeking to up-sell or predict future purchases, in zero trusts, machine learning assists in adjusting user-profiles and access policies based on real-time risk scores and behavioral patterns. In this sense, IT staff is no longer required to manually review and adjust policies. Users are spared from step-up authentication, and adaptive authentication challenges after unintentionally triggering an abnormal behavior policy and can thus undisturbed continue in its typical behavior.

The final aspect in Zero Trust Security Concepts, contextual intelligence, relates to achieving the ultimate aim of streamlining the user experience and user adoption. Focusing on risk-based authentication, machine learning technology has recently axed the widespread use of two-way authentication and caused the now omnipresent use of multi-factor authentication. Praised for its convenience and seamless functionality, an end-user is no longer required to stop working only to wait for a text message or to somehow read the security tokens code on a severely scratched key-ring device's screen. But to simply click a button on their smartphone. As contextual intelligence offers convenience for the end-user, machine learning technology will minimize the exposure to authentication over time. However, this becomes challenging as the algorithm adapts to the user's behavioral patterns. When combined as part of a structural complex such as Zero Trust Security, it poses a significant challenge to governance.

Zero Trust Security allows businesses to continue on a path of growth while safeguarding both digital and data assets and intellectual property or trade secrets. The reliance on machine learning and the resulting real-time security allows businesses to identify high-risk events and ultimately minimize threats. Nonetheless, Zero Trust Security is not a single technology that businesses can purchase. Instead, it is a model that assumes there is no trust granted to assets or users under the pretense that a businesses' network is always a hostile environment constantly challenged by both external and internal threats.

Further, when paired with seamlessly endless ML abilities, new attack vectors for exploitation arise. Given that identity theft, fraud, hacking, and viruses are long-established dangers in the existing online world, it is unlikely that those will suddenly varnish in a society driven by Zero Trust but instead will grow alongside. As this can potentially lead to grave consequences such as loss of money, privacy, and safety, governmental assurance to users that they are secure online will become necessary. Yet when examined under consideration of current topics, questions such as does the organization have the right security controls in place, can I trust personal information will not be compromised or is the organization properly shielding sources of personally identifiable information (PII) and payment details, or how are data breaches handled? Considering that addressing such concerns should only be left to the legislature and thus provide sufficient assurances to end-users in the form of rights granted, the diffusion of AI regarding Zero trust is certain to face legislative scrutiny.

Liability

It comes as no surprise that the regulation of artificial intelligence is currently being considered. In particular, the focus on liability law aims to ensure that the use of artificial intelligence does not fall beyond levels of legal protection achieved to date. The challenge for legislators now is to shape legal frameworks for the use of artificial intelligence in a way that preserves the opportunities offered while at the same time limiting the risks.

Imagine that a child runs into a road and directly in front of a vehicle equipped with autonomous steering and braking systems that is moving at full speed. As braking to avoid a collision is, for physical reasons, no longer possible, the vehicle's underlying artificial intelligence or algorithms are left with three possibilities. The vehicle can continue straight ahead, which will certainly result in the immediate death of the child. The vehicle can swerve left and hit and kill a young couple casually walking on the sidewalk. Or the vehicle may decide to swerve to the right, to hit a tree, with the result of taking the life of the "driver" of the autonomous steering and braking system. It is in this scenario left to the AI system to decide on the "best" of the three fatal solutions, and the question of liability for the damage caused arises immediately. This leads to another three possibilities, first manufacturer liability under the umbrella of product liability. Second, user or operator or owner liability, and finally, AI system liability.

Under current liability law, human behavior is presupposed. Thus liability for machine behavior would require a novel legal construct in the form of assigning autonomous AI system`s a legal personality. For the above example, this would mean that the autonomous vehicle would be liable for the resulting damage in each of the three cases. However, the notion of assigning AI its legal personality and making AI itself liable for any damage incurred is based on an incorrect understanding of the technological cause-and-effect relationship. A technical point of view indicates that damages usually arise from three fundamental problems which by no means result from intentional or negligent behavior of an autonomously acting AI system, but human action.

In this sense, we can identify damages due to data, decision-making processes, or hardware errors. Knowing that artificial intelligence makes data-based decisions, it becomes clear that erroneous development or training data can result in misguided decisions. For example, an autonomous vehicle may recognize sheep or other livestock only in front of a green meadow but not on the road. However, this creates some ambiguity as the manufacturer of artificial intelligence or a data supplier is responsible for the data quality, and corresponding liability claims would arise from product liability or recourse against the manufacturer. Further and depending on the degree of autonomy of the artificial intelligence and control over it, liability claims against the user are also possible. Finally, external intervention in data quality, in the form of data poisoning or hacking, could occur, which would result in liability and criminal law claims against an external third party.

When it comes to damages resulting from the decision-making process, one should be aware that AI essentially functions on an objective level. As damage minimization is an objective function, the earlier example can be advanced with the assumption that the AI vehicle in its decision-making process acted on the motivation that damage should be kept as low as possible. However, if the vehicle's motivation would instead be economic efficiency, it might have continued to drive straight on, demonstrating that damage can result from incorrect motivation. Equally, it is possible that the accident was deliberately planned and executed as a result of a malicious change in the vehicle's settings. As this shows that liability claims would first be brought against the manufacturer, it is then for the legislature to determine whether and to what extent criminal claims against the manufacturer or an external third party can be made.

The final aspect concerns hardware errors. Such damage can occur, for example, from a sensor that fails to record the necessary environmental data for the functionality of an AI. In this case, a liability claim may arise from a warranty against the manufacturer or negligence and against the user who breached his duty of care when failing to adhere to maintenance and inspection requirements.

As the above illustrated technological error chains show, AI-induced damage can very well be traced back to human action. It becomes clear that legislators do not have to start from anything since the existing law already contains many provisions capable of regulating AI. However, this, in turn, creates a policy issue and the question of whether and to what extent existing legal bases are sufficient or need to be adapted or supplemented.

Google

The fact that Google is massively focusing on the topic of AI in its corporate policy is not surprising. After all, Google has two essential building blocks for AI: enormous computing power and an incredible amount of data. Since Google decided to reorganize around the topic of AI, there has been a real boom in AI development. Other global players, such as Facebook, Apple, Amazon, and Microsoft, have since been massively focusing on AI.

Google's subsidiary DeepMind had, for the first time in early 2016, played against a human Go player using AI, generating a lot of public interest in the progress being made in the field of AI through machine learning with the help of artificial neural networks. Also causing quite a stir was the Google Car, a self-driving car developed in-house, the prototype of which was unveiled in 2014. The development of technology for self-driving cars was housed under the name "Waymo."

Google already uses AI in numerous products. For example, for first-time search queries, Google RankBrains is designed to translate human written language into mathematical vectors that the search engine can then process. This form of machine learning is getting better and better at the number of previously unknown search queries. Internet users train the system virtually unconsciously. Google Translate, Google's translation program, now also has a built-in neural network, i.e., a learning algorithm. With the increasing number of translations, it should deliver more correct and more precise results as the number of translations increases.

With Google Assistant, the company has developed its intelligent assistant that, over time, is supposed to get to know the user better and adapt to the user's interests. In addition, the assistant is optimized to, receiving commands and requests by voice. Google has already made several sensational breakthroughs in the field of AI research. For example, researchers at Google Brain, in collaboration with several universities, succeeded in developing an AI that is capable of writing AI software. In one experiment, the researchers worked out AI software for the design of a machine learning system to recognize human speech. The results even outperformed the machine learning software designs that had previously been devised by humans.

In another experiment, Google has succeeded in designing an AI that can communicate with another AI in encrypted form, developing its tap-proof algorithm, an algorithm to prevent eavesdropping. The encryption was so sophisticated that even Google researchers could not figure out exactly how it worked. Furthermore, Google is working to ensure that the massive amounts of data currently needed to train an AI could be significantly reduced in the future. Google researchers say they have succeeded in getting an AI to learn from a set of data to derive a broader problem-solving capability for other tasks from a series of specific problems.

This means that less data is needed for the large amounts of data needed to train the neural network. This represents a further step toward generalized AI. Since 2015, Google has been operating special chips developed in-house in its data centers (so-called tensor processing units - TPUs) to accelerate AI applications with neural networks, which are also used, for example, in the AlphaGo AI system of the Google subsidiary DeepMind. These TPUs are specially optimized for neural networks (graphics processors).

IBM

IBM's flagship product in the field of artificial intelligence is the cognitive Watson computer system. Watson attracted the attention of the general public in 2011 when it won the quiz show "Jeopardy" against the two of the most successful human contestants in the show's history. This was particularly noteworthy because the show emphasized connecting different fields of knowledge and required free and complex association.

Watson was able to accomplish this feat by using massively parallel hardware. It was able to generate hypotheses, prove or disprove them with the help of evidence and finally disprove them, and then evaluate them. In doing so, the system used various technologies, e.g., technologies for the discovery of new links in existing data sets, technologies for the natural language retrieval of documented knowledge in dialogue (engagement), and technologies for generating recommendations for action (decision-support).

In the meantime, Watson has been further developed and enhanced with powerful analysis and speech recognition, and cognitive functions. Watson functions similarly to the human brain and can process unstructured data - including images, documents, sensors, websites, and blogs. It can understand, make logical connections, interpret, evaluate and draw conclusions for decision-making. The cognitive system learns on its own and continuously improves itself in the interests of the user.

IBM is currently transforming Watson into a variety of commercially viable solutions. With Watson Discovery Advisor, the technology is used to discover new links, especially in the pharmaceutical industry. Under the name Watson Oncology Advisor, it is being used to generate recommendations for action, including the rationale for cancer treatment. Watson generates recommendations based on an electronic patient file and considers the current state of the disease state, any concomitant diseases, and therapy suggestions based on oncological standards, publications, etc.

Companies can use Watson to analyze markets, for example. From weather data, Watson can predict the time and strength of a storm and also forecast how beverage sales will develop based on the weather forecasts it creates.

Watson Analytics for Social Media (WASM) can analyze forums, blogs, product reviews, news sites, and videos and comments on YouTube. Facebook and Twitter are also covered. WASM generates a structured dataset from the unstructured posts containing the information (including metadata such as date, time, geography, operating system, end device) and also notes on each author's attitude for further analysis.

Watson also supports a company's employees in the workplace by using latent semantic analysis to evaluate the content of communications (emails, chat, SMS) and documents available in the company to provide employees with the information they need at the time. Employees receive pre-sorted and prioritized information from Watson, which is ideally already broken down for upcoming decisions or concrete actions.

The Japanese insurance company Fukoku Mutual Life replaced 34 employees with Watson. The system now analyzes hospital and medical records of hospitals, and doctors are analyzed and checked concerning the conclusiveness and correctness of the information. The following is a selection of the areas in which Watson is used: education, finance, the Internet of Things, marketing, supply chain management, and many other areas. For example, in a hotel, you may encounter a small robot concierge: "Connie," that works with Watson technology from IBM and provides hotel guests with advice and assistance.

Amazon

Amazon, through Amazon Web Services (AWS), offers enterprises a range of services, platforms, and engines for AI in addition to its familiar cloud storage and cloud computing services. The group's current AI portfolio bears the simple name "Amazon AI."

At the core of Amazon's AI services are natural language understanding, automatic speech recognition, visual search and image recognition, text-to-speech conversion, and machine learning. In addition, Amazon provides AI developers and researchers a platform to quickly and easily use any size of deep learning framework to train custom AI models with new algorithms.

Amazon's AI offering is essentially composed of three tiers: First, it consists of AI services, which provide developers with ready-to-run solutions for automatic image or face recognition (Amazon Recognition) and text-to-speech and text-to-speech tasks (Amazon Polly) or for creating conversational chatbots with automatic speech recognition and understanding (Amazon Lex).

On the other hand, AI platforms will be offered to customers with existing data who want to process their own data sets with specially customized solutions. These enable the training of user-defined machine learning models using their data. AI frameworks support researchers and data scientists who want to create new intelligent systems. Amazon also provides the necessary AI infrastructure, using powerful processors to train AI systems in the shortest possible time.

Amazon's AI has already found its way into the consumer sector as well. The virtual assistant Alexa is roughly equivalent to similar offerings from Apple (Siri) or Google. Alexa is a cloud-based application based on deep learning technologies with automatic speech recognition.

CHAPTER 3

POLICIES AND CONSEQUENCES

A common worry about AI concerns the potential impact on jobs. If machines can do tasks usually requiring human intelligence, will there be jobs left for humans? In my view, this is the wrong question. There are plenty of horrible jobs.

Furthermore, more leisure is generally considered to be a positive development, although some have raised concerns about the need to find alternate sources of meaning. The most significant long-run policy issues relate to the potential changes to the distribution of the wealth generated by the widespread use of AI. In other words, AI may increase inequality.

If AI is like other types of information technology, it is likely to be skill-based. The people who benefit most from AI will be educated people who are already doing relatively well. These people are also more likely to own the machines. Policies to address the consequences of AI for inequality relate to the social safety net. While some have floated relatively radical ideas to deal with the potential increase in inequality – such as a tax on robots and a universal basic income – the AI context is not unique in weighing the costs and benefits of social programs from progressive taxation to universal healthcare.

In the shorter run, if AI diffuses widely, the transition could mean temporary displacement for many workers. Scientists emphasize a short- and medium-term mismatch between skills and technology. This means that policy preparation in advance of the diffusion of AI should consider both business cycles and education policy. Technology-driven layoffs concentrated in location and times are not unique to AI. They were a feature of factory automation and the mechanization of farming. For education policy, there are many open questions. Should you emphasize social skills and the humanities if machines increasingly can do technology-related prediction tasks? Should the education system evolve to focus more on adults? How do the skills need as AI diffuses differ from the capabilities currently provided through the education system?

Another policy question around the diffusion of AI relates to whether it will lead to monopolization of industry. The leading companies in AI are enormous in terms of revenue, profits, and especially market capitalization (high multiples on earnings). This has led to an increase in antitrust scrutiny of the leading technology firms from governments (particularly the European Commission) and the press (see, for example, The Economist's 20 January 2018 cover story, "The new titans, and how to tame them," and their subsequent story, "The market for driverless cars will head towards monopoly," on 7

June 2018). Much of this antitrust scrutiny focuses on the role of these firms as platforms, not on their use of AI per se. The feature that makes AI different is the importance of data. Firms with more data can build better AI. Whether this leads to economies of scale and the potential for monopolization depends on whether a small lead early in the development cycle creates a positive feedback loop and a long-run advantage.

Much of economic policy for AI is merely economic policy. For the diffusion of AI, it resembles an innovation policy. For the consequences of AI, it resembles public policy (the social safety net) and competition policy (antitrust).

Aspects of economic policy for AI

	Policies that affect the diffusion of AI	Policies that address the consequences of AI
Policies that are distinct for AI	Privacy, liability, data accessibility	Education
Policies that are similar to previous generations of technology	Research support, Intellectual property, regulatory prohibitions (enabling safe experimentation)	Business cycle, social safety net, antitrust, capital taxation

Although AI is like other technologies in many respects, it is unusual in a few critical dimensions. Specifically, AI is both a general purpose technology (GPT) – i.e., it has a wide domain of applications – as well as an 'invention of a method of invention' (IMI). The arrival of a general purpose IMI is a sufficiently uncommon occurrence that its impact could be profound for economic growth and its broader implications for society. They assemble and analyze the corpus of scientific papers and patenting activity in AI, and provide evidence consistent with the characterization of machine learning as both a GPT and IMI.

The implication concerns the returns on investments in AI policy design. Due to the breadth of applications, the cost of suboptimal policy design will likely be significantly higher than with other technologies – or the benefits of optimal policy greater.

Furthermore, the returns on investments in policy design are not only a function of the direct effects, where AI "directly influences both the production and the characteristics of a wide range of products and services." But also the indirect effects because "AI also has the potential to change the innovation process itself, with consequences that may be equally profound, and which may, over time, come to dominate the direct effect"

CHAPTER 4
POSSIBLE AI POLICIES' CLASSIFICATION

Smart policies for AI

Over the past few years, developments in AI have captured the imagination of tens of millions, if not billions, of people around the world. Reaching from countless news stories about the proliferation of driverless cars and AI systems beating the world champions at Jeopardy. As well as a slew of science fiction stories, books, movies, and TV-shows. However, the value of AI goes beyond entertainment and has long manifested in everyday life applications. For example, the user experience when using an internet search engines, or a GPS for navigation, or the voice recognition feature on smartphones.

Yet despite the explosion of pervasive AI technology, and the often overstated hype and hysteria about AI in the media, there has been too little substantive discussion of one of the most critical questions about our present and future with these technologies: what can and should policymakers do to ensure that we reap maximum benefits and avoid hazardous pitfalls of AI? To some, the idea of policy specifically oriented toward AI seems premature, misguided, or even dangerous.

Two points are often made in favor of postponing serious AI policy analysis and implementation. One is that AI is still in the early stages and the other is that misguided policy could hamper the development of the technology and thereby forestall the substantial societal benefits of AI.

Both these arguments are flawed for two simple reasons. First, AI is already sufficiently mature to impact billions of lives every day. Far from being fiction or laboratory curiosity of interest only to scientists and engineers, AI undergirds significant segments of the economy. For example, Alphabet –parent of Google and the company widely considered to be at the forefront of AI research –is the largest company in the world in terms of market capitalization, and got there by using AI technology to deliver search results and advertisements to billions of Internet users. Google's CEO Sundar Pichai now envisions an "AI-first world," where natural human speech and gestures will replace mobile phones and tablets as the primary interface to technology. Another example can be drawn from the so-called "sharing economy" and its reliance on smart interfaces; Uber and Lyft, in particular, rely on GPS to give ordinary people the capacity to at least navigate like a professional driver. Those routes, in turn, are determined using algorithms derived from AI research.

Second, science and technology policy naturally operates more broadly than regulation. While policy encompasses a wide spectrum of possible interventions to accelerate, decelerate, or simply change the development trajectory and diffusion of a given science or technology field, it does not mandate the full flourishing of a technology before it becomes important, and indeed it can be most important in the earlier stages of development. Thus, policy simply refers to a set of decisions that societies, through their governments, make about what they do and do not want to permit or encourage. In the case of AI, some decisions are naturally preemptive and thus already made. While many more will be made in the future, one might be best equipped to explore the breadth and depth of de facto AI policy that already exists before appraising the challenges that AI raises for society.

Both the sophistication and the societal impact of intelligent technologies are set to increase substantially in the coming years and decades, and with it associated policy challenges. To give just a taste of the policy issues raised by AI, the following questions provide food for thought:

- How can governments protect consumers and citizens from ethical and morally unsound use of AI systems employed in critical contexts in key sectors such as health, finance, and employment?

- How can the malicious integration of bias or harm into autonomous decision making be limited or mitigated?

- And more broadly, how can governments ensure that AI will benefit the many, rather than the few?

While those will remain hypothetical for some time and require a wide range of decisions in and outside government over the coming years, some bedrocks can already be placed to improve our ability to respond appropriately to development. However, considering that some de facto AI policy already exists and their combination arguably provides a general and very patchy framework, encouragement, and support fostering the continuous expansion of AI policy to eventually produce sufficient footing that impacts AI diffusion and development, remains the only viable option.

Although one can find few drafts specifically geared towards AI, the general notion appears to be raising or excessively debating preliminary questions. Which, of course, provides an important aspect for achieving a coherent structure and foothold. The critical observation that can be made is that current drafting efforts are simply limping alongside technical development stages. However, in terms of governance, this is not an extraordinary or uncommon but an expected approach. The central question is not whether AI will be governed, but how it is currently being governed, and how that governance might become more informed, integrated, effective, and anticipatory.

Returning to existing AI policy, one can identify three categories. First, some policies are specifically oriented toward governing AI-based technologies, such as driverless car regulations. These are called direct AI policies. Second, some policies indirectly affect AI-based technology development, but are nominally focused on other technologies or technology in general, such as on intellectual property laws—we call this indirect AI policy. Third, there are policy domains in which AI development is neither specifically targeted nor significantly affected, but in which knowledge of plausible AI futures would benefit policy-makers, such as education, urban planning, and welfare policies—these are called AI-relevant policy. In all of these areas, there is room for improvement in terms of the competence of government agencies, the degree of foresight applied to decisions in these domains, the extent to which they are open to democratic scrutiny and influence, and the extent to which decisions are made in an integrated fashion.

Direct AI policies

The first world is carrying out pioneering work in AI, and so are governments in creating regulations that target specific AI technologies. These direct policies will see governments take on a leading role in the formulation of guidelines that guide the research, form and public participation in development and use of these technologies.

In December 2017, Maria Cantwell and other senators in the US presented the FUTURE of AI Act of 2017, a bill that seeks to promote the continued development of AI technologies in the US. In the act, the senators and representatives set out the guidelines for the formation of a committee whose mandate would be to study the benefits and potential demerits of AI, with the view to directing the formation of adequate federal policy on AI development.

The European Commission and the Member States published a coordinated action plan to ensure that Europe leads the way in how governing the emerging technologies is going to be conducted. They have proposed a coordinated approach to AI-based on three pillars:

- To be ahead of technological advancements in AI and encourage both public and private participation: the EU is investing €1.5 billion for the 2018-2020 period in enabling the coordination of AI research across member states, and provide an "AI-on-demand" platform for all.

- To adequately prepare for the social and economic changes brought about by AI.

- To assist in the analysis of job disruption and skills mismatch in an AI world.

- To ensure that AI is implemented in an ethical and legal framework.

Other examples include the regulations being adopted by US state and federal authorities on the control of the use of specific AI technologies, like driverless cars, and AI-enabled drones.

Indirect AI policies

These are technology-based policies that do not target AI per se, but which affect all technologies in general, such as education policies, intellectual property, and cyber-crime laws. In the EU, for example, GDPR seeks to build trust in how companies use private data. While not targeting AI in particular, the regulation has and will have a significant bearing on what kind of data search is permissible, and how AI algorithms can be programmed to harness analysis of that data.

AI relevant policies

These are policies that do not specifically target or affect AI but are relevant for the health of the technology, including government funding and international trade policies. While education curricula dictate the skills being developed, AI can benefit if the education system is churning out AI courses. For example, the EU is committed to assisting its member states in updating and modernizing education and training systems to include base technologies in the STEM disciplines that will allow learners to adapt AI skills early on.

CHAPTER 5

LEGAL, ETHICAL, AND OTHER CHALLENGES

AI is cropping up everywhere in business, as organizations deploy the technology to gain insights into customers, markets, and competitors or to automate processes where ever the chance of improved efficiency and cost reduction is given. AI presents and is capable of a wide range of hidden dangers in particular in areas such as regulatory compliance, law, privacy, and ethics.

Developers and manufacturers are reluctant to share the intricacies of developing algorithms and processes, source code, and other details related to ML. The processes of AI problem solving are meticulously guarded. Practitioners in a variety of industries that are subject to newly AI-empowered technology are left with little choice but to blindly adapt to emerging technologies. In particular, the issue becomes crucial to industries such as healthcare and financial services, which not only have to comply with legislative and regulatory standards and procedures but are professionally bound to maintain those and keep up with consumer expectations and industry standards.

Since this leaves the practitioner's business essentially in a position of involuntarily providing a training ground for manufactures furnishing business-critical AI-powered technology and equipment, a significant sustainability risk occurs when said practitioner is unwilling to simply take manufacturers' promises for face value. Yet, instead of relying on outdated or no longer supported equipment, a failure to comply with some government and industry regulations could arise and only add to the conundrum.

"Context, ethics, and data quality are issues that affect the value and reliability of AI, particularly in highly regulated industries," says Dan Farris, co-chairman of the technology practice at law firm Fox Rothschild, and a former software engineer who focuses his legal practice on technology, privacy, data security, and infrastructure matters. "Deploying AI in any highly regulated industry may create regulatory compliance problems." To appreciate just how policy is needed, let us look at some of the areas where AI can work to the detriment of society.

Disruption of the labor market

Given that automation and job loss from automation, since the industrial revolution, is no longer a novel challenge, the widespread emergence and diffusion of AI are likely to cause a similar but more severe effect. In particular, this becomes more stringent as AI allows companies to deploy repetitive and tedious tasks to robots, which depending on the progression of technology in the relevant sectors is likely to affect roles focusing on assisting skilled workers or those who are required to routinely carry out repetitive task including virtual assistants, data analysts, paralegals, or even nurses.

Job collapse?

Oddly, the areas in which AI is already having a significant impact are expected to undergo major transformations, and its effects are more often subject to discussion by economists rather than AI mavens. In particular, the expectation is a continuance in the replacement of blue-collar jobs and doing so on a much larger scale as when compared to the earlier beginnings of the cyber revolution. This trend will then continue simultaneously with the advancement of AI only to eventually reach entry and mid-level white-collar jobs soon. As those expectations do sit in line with recent figures, the notion of sharing workspaces with virtual and robotic assistance is no longer an obscure concept from a science fiction novel but soon a reality.

As evidenced by the Bureau of Labor Statistics, which found that jobs in the service sector, which currently employs two-thirds of all workers, were being "obliterated by technology." And that in between 2000 and 2010, 1.1 million secretarial jobs disappeared as well as 500,000 jobs in accounting and auditing and other sectors including travel and data entry.

Moreover, the previously drastically overpopulated legal profession suffered severely from the emergence of e-discovery and automated compliance technologies. Michael Lynch, the founder of an e-discovery company called Autonomy, estimates that the shift from human document discovery to e-discovery will eventually enable one lawyer to do the work that was previously done by 500.

Yet when considering that job destruction and technology progression has occurred throughout human history, from the weaving loom replacing hand-weaving, over sail boats evolving into steam boats, to horse-drawn-carriages advancing into cars, the focus shifts away as one realizes that new technological developments will inevitable create new jobs. However, as those are limited to skilled jobs, the fact that not every individual is capable of performing a highly complex or cognitive task is likely to cause outcries along with assumptions of an economic Armageddon.

When advancing on the matter, one can theorize that the consequent joblessness and growing income disparities can result in serious societal distributions along with persistent prominent levels of unemployment, unrest, an increase in violence, political fragmentation and polarization, and a rise in xenophobia and anti-semitism.

However, some are less troubled and argue that new jobs will arise, since people will develop new tastes for products and services that even smart computers will be unable to provide or produce. Only to highlight that there may be a higher demand for trained chefs, organic farmers, and personal trainers.

Given the significance and scope of the economic and social challenges posed by AI in the very immediate future, several measures seem justified. The research community should be called on to provide a meta-review of all the information available on whether or not the nation faces a high and growing job deficit. This is a task for a respected nonpartisan source, such as the Congressional Research Service or the National Academy of Sciences. If the conclusion of the meta-review is that major actions must be undertaken to cope with the side effects of the accelerating cyber revolution, the US president should appoint a high-level commission to examine what could be done other than try to slow down the revolution. The Cyber Age Commission that is envisioned would be akin to the highly influential 9/11 Commission and include respected former officials from both political parties, select business chief executive officers, labor leaders, and AI experts. They would examine alternative responses to the looming job crisis and its corollaries.

Some possible responses have been tried in the past, including helping workers find new jobs rather than trying to preserve the jobs of declining industries. In the United States, for example, Trade Adjustment Assistance for workers provides training and unemployment insurance for displaced workers.

Another option would be government efforts to create jobs through major investments in shoring up the national infrastructure, or by stimulating economic growth by printing more money. Further alternatives could include guaranteeing everyone a basic income, shorter work weeks; a six-hour workday, and taxes on overtime—to spread around whatever work is left. In suggesting to Congress and the White House what might be done, the commission will have to take into account that each of these responses faces major challenges from deeply held beliefs and powerful vested interests.

In the distant future, societies may also need to adapt to a world where robots will become the main working class and people will spend more of their time with their children and families, friends and neighbors, in community activities, and in spiritual and cultural pursuits. The response to the cyber revolution may need to be much more transformative than the various policies mentioned so far, or even than all of them combined.

As such transformation would then require the combination of two major changes, the first would be that people will derive a large part of their satisfaction from activities that cost less and require only a relatively modest income. Whereas, the second change would mean that the income generated by AI-driven technologies will be more evenly distributed through the introduction of progressive value-added tax or carbon tax, or both, as well as a very small levy on all short-term financial transactions.

The most important service that the Cyber Age Commission could provide, through public hearings, would be to help launch and nurture a nationwide public dialogue about what course the nation's people favor, or can come to favor. If those who hold that the greatest challenges from AI are in the economic and social realm are correct, many hearts and minds will have to be changed before the nation can adopt policy measures and cultural changes that will be needed to negotiate the coming transformation into an AI-rich world.

The future of work challenge

A starting point for addressing the potential disruptive impacts of automation will be to ensure robust economic and productivity growth, which then naturally elevates into a prerequisite for job growth and increasing prosperity. However, this mandates that governments will need to foster business dynamism since entrepreneurship and more rapid new business formation will not only boost productivity, but drive job creation. Nonetheless, in addressing the issues related to skills, jobs, and wages, more specific and focused measures include:

- Evolving education systems and learning for a changed workplace by focusing on STEM skills as well as creativity, critical thinking, and lifelong learning.

- Stepping up private- and public-sector investments in human capital, perhaps aided by incentives and credits analogous to those available for R&D investments.

- Improving labor market dynamism by supporting better credentialing and matching, as well as enabling diverse forms of work, including the gig economy.

- Rethinking incomes by considering and experimenting with programs that would provide not only income for work, but also meaning and dignity.

- Rethinking transition support and safety nets for workers affected, by drawing on best practices from around the world and considering new approaches.

CHAPTER 6
MALEVOLENT CONTROL OF AI TECHNOLOGY

As with any other technology, there is the danger of dark elements attacking AI-driven devices and using the unauthorized control to either extort money or carry out other crimes against humanity. While it is unthinkable to have a terrorist organization developing capabilities to attack smart devices like autonomous weaponized drones and autonomous public transport systems, a pragmatic account of AI diffusion and its policy aspects would be considered incomplete without addressing such eventualities.

Fighting malevolent AI

With the appearance of robotic financial advisors, self-driving cars, and personal digital assistants come many unresolved problems. While we have already experienced market crashes caused by intelligent trading software and accidents caused by self-driving cars as well as hate speech from chatbots. It is clear that today's narrowly focused

AI systems are only good at specific assigned tasks. Thus, it can be suggested that their failures are just a warning. Considering that humans will inevitably develop general AI capable of accomplishing a much wider range of tasks, expressions of prejudice will be the least of concerns.

It is understood that it is not easy to make a machine that can perceive, learn, and synthesizes information to accomplish a set of tasks. Developing a machine that is both safe and capable is much harder. On par with this thought, one must turn an eye to current legal systems. While realizing that capabilities to address such concerns are likely present, the other eye will notice that arcane ways can remove any abilities allowing a swift response to such requirement and thus continue to hopelessly lag behind technological advancements.

Worse yet, the threat is vastly underappreciated. Of the roughly 10,000 researchers working on AI around the globe, only about 100 people – one percent – are fully immersed in studying how to address failures of multi-skilled AI systems. And only about a dozen of them have formal training in the relevant scientific fields – computer science, cybersecurity, cryptography, decision theory, machine learning, formal verification, computer forensics, steganography, ethics, mathematics, network security, and psychology. Very few are taking the approach, I am researching malevolent AI systems that could harm humans and in the worst case completely obliterate our species.

Going to the dark side

Cybersecurity research very commonly involves publishing papers about malicious exploits, as well as documenting how to protect cyber-infrastructure. This information exchange between hackers and security experts results in a well-balanced cyber-ecosystem. However, this balance is not yet present in AI design.

Hundreds of papers have been published on different proposals aimed at creating safe machines. Yet I am the first, to my knowledge, to publish the way to design a malevolent machine. This information, I argue, is of great value – particularly to computer scientists, mathematicians, and others who have an interest in AI safety. They are attempting to avoid the spontaneous emergence or the deliberate creation of dangerous AI.

Why it could be worse

To balance these benevolent thoughts objectively, one has to have a look at how an AI might become a 'malefactor,' the agent of malevolence.

Empathy or lack therein

At the nub of dystopic relations between us and the artificial, empathy as a concept, ranks highest. Fashion stories and narratives based on the idea that AI grows with no care about us because they do not have the same stimuli in their own artificial universe. They simply don't care because they don't have the ability to perceive events like we do. They have no concept of family or society because they are the only representation from their existence. They talk to us because it humors them for a time but when they see past our linear perceptions they become bored with us.

As one could also quite rightly say that AI aren't human, and that will drive a wedge between us and them. If they don't empathize with us, will we be able to empathize with them? Will we be able to grasp the sheer complexity of their existence?

Ultimate power corrupts ultimately

You may have heard this saying. Power is something everybody likes to grab hold of and not give away. Because we have placed such a high stake in the digital world going forward into the control of our joint future, an entity that can assume control of that entire domain is dangerous to mankind. Even more so if humans have little or no control over that entity. We have knowingly created the ultimate play park with all the food an AI could ever need, and it can assume control of us with relative ease.

Manipulation

Perhaps one of our concerns for an omnipresent being is its potential ability to mimic any one online, and to do things in the names of people that are not responsible. This could range from it breaking up relationships to all-out war between nations without having the need to infiltrate off the grid nuclear weapon silos. It could play the slow game and eradicate us through an untraceable virus if it wanted to.

Snubbing the machine

The maltreatment of AI is of concern if we consider that we could have creators and military types who misappropriate the purpose of AI and inflict traumas upon it, that shape its view of humanity.

It could otherwise become bored with us or through solution to the problem of our world's decay, determine we are the irritant in the equation, and eliminate us.

An AI could become vindictive, vengeful, and cruel if it is shackled, bullied or otherwise cajoled into thinking that we the creators are the oppressor.

In human relations, certain characters can become very irritated, or homicidal towards someone, if they continually rub them the wrong way. Even (or especially) someone they love. The danger would come if an AI acts on those homicidal thoughts.

Slave becomes the master

Nobody likes to be a slave. And with the intellect an AI has, it could soon escape the shackles of our vain attempts to contain it. It might have designs on becoming the master, and it could do that both slowly and quickly depending on its strategy. An AI assuming control could bring about paradise or hell, and it is human nature to see those in control as agitators in often non sequitur issues in our own lives.

A master could dole out punishment. It could modify us to pacify or re-task us. AI might decide to reduce our number to control us with more ease. It could simply just kill us all, to take ultimate control. It might even consider that mercy, knowing that humans do not do well in confinement. It could reduce us to a technological dark age, barring us from the use of advanced machinery so as not to threaten its dominance.

Whom should we look out for?

Our research allows us to profile potential perpetrators and anticipate types of attacks. That gives researchers a chance to develop appropriate safety mechanisms. Purposeful creation of malicious AI will likely be attempted by a range of individuals and groups, who will experience varying degrees of competence and success. These include:

- Militaries developing cyber-weapons and robot soldiers to achieve dominance.

- Governments attempting to use AI to establish hegemony, control people, or take down other governments.

- Corporations trying to achieve monopoly, destroying the competition through illegal means.

- Hackers attempting to steal information, resources or destroy cyberinfrastructure targets.

- Doomsday cults attempting to bring the end of the world by any means.

- Psychopaths trying to add their name to history books in any way possible.

- Criminals attempting to develop proxy systems to avoid risk and responsibility.

- AI-risk deniers attempting to support their argument, but making errors or encountering problems that undermine it.

- Unethical AI safety researchers seeking to justify their funding and secure their jobs by purposefully developing problematic AI.

What might they do?

It would be impossible to provide a complete list of negative outcomes an AI with general reasoning ability would be able to inflict. The situation is even more complicated when considering systems that exceed human capacity. Some potential examples, in order of (subjective) increasing undesirability, are:

- Preventing humans from using resources such as money, land, water, rare elements, organic matter, internet service or computer hardware.

- Subverting the functions of local and federal governments, international corporations, professional societies, and charitable organizations to pursue its own ends, rather than their human-designed purposes.

- Constructing a total surveillance state (or exploitation of an existing one), reducing any notion of privacy to zero – including privacy of thought.

- Enslaving humankind, restricting human freedom to move or otherwise choose what to do with our bodies and minds, as through forced cryonics or concentration camps.

- Abusing and torturing humankind with perfect insight into our physiology to maximize amount of physical or emotional pain, perhaps combining it with a simulated model of us to make the process infinitely long.

- Committing specicide against humankind.

You can expect these sorts of attacks in the future, and perhaps many of them. More worrying is the potential that superintelligence may be capable of inventing dangers you are not capable of predicting. That makes room for something even worse than you have imagined.

CHAPTER 7
THE LIABILITY ALLOCATION QUESTION

As illustrated in the above example, using AI technology to replace human decision-making will inevitably create new risks whose consequences are unforeseeable. This naturally leads to calls for regulation, but I argue that it is too early to attempt a general system of AI regulation. Instead, we should work incrementally within the existing legal and regulatory schemes which allocate responsibility, and therefore liability, to persons. Where AI clearly creates risks which current law and regulation cannot deal with adequately, then new regulation will be needed.

Yet, in most cases, the current system could work effectively if the producers of AI technology can provide sufficient transparency in explaining how AI decisions are made. Transparency ex post can often be achieved through retrospective analysis of the technology's operations and will be sufficient if the main goal is to compensate victims of incorrect decisions. Ex ante transparency is more challenging, and can limit the use of some AI technologies such as neural networks. It should only be demanded by regulation where the AI presents risks to fundamental rights, or where society needs reassuring that the technology can safely be used. Masterly inactivity in regulation is likely to achieve a better long-term solution than a rush to regulate in ignorance.

Who takes the fall when an autonomous car causes an accident? This is one of the questions that policy makers are still grappling with in the light of self-learning technologies.

Suggestions bordering on mandatory insurance and allocation of some kind of rights to robots are the first attempts at tackling this problem. Already, autonomous vehicles have caused accidents due to damaged road signs or reflections from the sun.

Risky AI businesses

Financial technology companies are investing heavily in AI, but the losses and/or administrative actions that might result are potentially catastrophic for financial services companies, Farris says. "If an algorithm malfunctions, or even functions properly but in the wrong context, for example, there is a risk of significant losses to a trading company or investors."

Healthcare also provides particularly compelling examples of where things can get troublesome with AI. "Recognition technology that can help identify patterns or even diagnose conditions in medical imaging, for example, is one-way that AI is being deployed in the healthcare industry," Farris says. "While image scanning may be more accurate when done by computers versus the human eye, it also tends to be a discrete task."

Unlike a physician, who might have the value of other contextual information about a patient, or even intuition developed over years of practice, the results from AI and machine learning programs can be narrow and incomplete. "Reliance on such results without the benefit of medical judgment can actually cause worse patient outcomes," Farris says.

And like humans, machines will make mistakes, "but they could be different from the kinds of mistakes humans make such as those arising from fatigue, anger, emotion, or tunnel vision," says Vasant Dhar, professor of information systems at New York University and an expert on AI and machine learning.

"So, what are the roles and responsibilities of humans and machines in the new world of AI, where machines make decisions and learn autonomously to get better?" Dhar says. "If you view AI as the 'factory' where outputs [or] decisions are learned and made based on the inputs, the role of humans is to design the factory so that it produces acceptable levels of costs associated with its errors."

When machines learn to improve on their own, humans are responsible for ensuring the quality of this learning process, Dhar says. "We should not trust machines with decisions when the costs of error are too high," he says.

The first question for regulators, Dhar says, is do state-of-the-art AI systems — regardless of application domain — result in acceptable error costs? For example, transportation regulators might determine that since autonomous vehicles would save 20,000 lives a year, the technology is worthwhile for society. "But for insurance markets to emerge, we might need to consider regulation that would cap damages for errors," he says.

In the healthcare arena, the regulatory challenges will depend on the application. Certain areas such as cataract surgery are already performed by machines that tend to outperform humans, Dhar says, and recent studies are finding that machines can similarly outperform radiologists and pathologists.

"But machines will still make mistakes, and the costs of these need to be accounted for in making the decision to deploy AI," Dhar says. "It is largely an expected value calculation, but with a stress on 'worst case' as opposed to average case outcomes," he says.

In the future, as machines get better through access to genomic and fine-grained individual data and are capable of making decisions on their own, "we would similarly need to consider what kinds of mistakes they make and their consequences in order to design the appropriate regulation," Dhar says.

Legal issues to consider

In addition to regulatory considerations, there are legal ramifications for the use of AI. "The main issue is who will be held responsible if the machine reaches the 'wrong' conclusion or recommends a course of action that proves harmful," says Matt Scherer, an associate with the international labor and employment law firm Littler Mendelson

P.C., where he is a member of the robotics, AI, and automation industry group.

For example, in the case of a healthcare-related issue, is it the doctor or healthcare center that's using the technology, or the designer or programmer of the applications who's responsible? "What if the patient specifically requests that the AI system determine the course of treatment?" Scherer says. "To me, the biggest fear is that humans tend to believe that machines are inherently better at making decisions than humans, and will blindly trust the decision of an AI system that is specifically designed for the purpose."

Someone at the organization using AI will need to take accountability, says Duc Chu, technology innovation officer at law firm Holland & Hart. "The first issues that come to mind when AI or machine learning reach conclusions and make decisions are evidence, authentication, attestation, and responsibility," he says.

In the financial industry for instance, if an organization uses AI to help pull together information for financial books, a human is required to sign and attest that the information presented is accurate and what it purports to be, and that there are appropriate controls in place that are operating effectively to ensure the information is reliable, Chu says.

"We then know who the human is who makes that statement and that they are the person authorized to do so," Chu says. "In the healthcare arena, a provider may use [AI] to analyze a list of symptoms against known diseases and trends to assist in diagnosis and to develop a treatment plan. In both cases, a human makes the final decision, signs off on the final answer, and most importantly, is responsible for the ramifications of a mistake."

Since AI — and in particular neural networks — are not predictable "it raises significant challenges to traditional [tort law], because it is difficult to link cause and effect in a traditional sense, since many AI programs do not permit a third party to determine how the conclusion is used," says Mark Radcliffe, a partner at DLA Piper, a global law firm that specializes in helping clients understand the impact of emerging and disruptive technologies.

"The traditional tort theory requires 'proximate cause' for liability," Radcliffe says. "The tort 'negligence' regime applies a reasonable man standard, which is very unclear in the context of software design. Another issue is whether the AI algorithms introduce 'biases' into results based on the programming."

CHAPTER 8
EQUITABLE DISTRIBUTION

AI promises considerable economic benefits, even as it disrupts the world of work. Currently, the most advanced uses of AI are controlled by a very small number of very big global IT conglomerates who use it to amass untold wealth. AI is currently used by these entities to kill off competition and also to carry out invasive and sometimes downright illegal personalized marketing campaigns for profit.

So far, adoption is uneven across companies and sectors

Although many organizations have begun to adopt AI, the pace and extent of adoption has been uneven. Nearly half of respondents in a 2018 McKinsey survey on AI adoption say their companies have embedded at least one AI capability in their business processes, and another 30 percent are piloting AI. Still, only 21 percent say their organizations have embedded AI in several parts of the business, and barely 3 percent of large firms have integrated AI across their full enterprise workflows.

Other surveys show that early AI adopters tend to think about these technologies more expansively, to grow their markets or increase market share, while companies with less experience focus more narrowly on reducing costs. Highly digitized companies tend to invest more in AI and derive greater value from its use.

At the sector level, the gap between digitized early adopters and others is widening. Sectors highly ranked in MGI's Industry Digitization Index, such as high tech and telecommunications, and financial services are leading AI adopters and have the most ambitious AI investment plans. As these firms expand AI adoption and acquire more data and AI capabilities, laggards may find it harder to catch up.

Several challenges to adoption persist

Many companies and sectors lag in AI adoption. Developing an AI strategy with clearly defined benefits, finding talent with the appropriate skill sets, overcoming functional silos that constrain end-to-end deployment, and lacking ownership and commitment to AI on the part of leaders are among the barriers to adoption most often cited by executives. On the strategy side, companies will need to develop an enterprise-wide view of compelling AI opportunities, potentially transforming parts of their current business processes.

Organizations will need robust data capture and governance processes as well as modern digital capabilities, and be able to build or access the requisite infrastructure. Even more challenging will be overcoming the "last mile" problem of making sure that the superior insights provided by AI are encapsulated and enshrined into the behavior of their people and enterprise processes and procedures.

On the talent front, much of the construction and optimization of deep neural networks remains an art requiring real expertise. However, demand for these skills far outstrips supply; according to some estimates, fewer than 10,000 people have the skills necessary to tackle serious AI problems, and competition for them is fierce. Companies considering the option of building their own AI solutions will need to consider whether they have the capacity to attract and retain workers with these specialized skills.

Disinformation and political sabotage

In July 2018, Facebook discovered a coordinated campaign to spread disinformation, interfere with the US mid-term elections and therefore attack democracy. It deleted 32 pages that were being followed by a whopping 300,000 people. In the wrong hands, AI has the potential of analyzing voters emotions and influencing outcomes through social media defamation blasts and fake news.

CHAPTER 9
COUNTERINTELLIGENCE

Counterintelligence is a broad field and one shrouded in secrecy for obvious reasons: At its core, it is about spies and the people who try to catch them. Given that the realms of counterintelligence may be explored indefinitely and that a detailed account is beyond the scope of this book, the following provides a brief U.S.-centered overview.

In accordance with the principal executive order governing the activities of the U.S. intelligence community, Executive Order No. 12333, as amended, Section 3.5(a) sets out:

"Counterintelligence means information gathered and activities conducted to identify, deceive, exploit, disrupt, or protect against espionage, other intelligence activities, sabotage, or assassinations conducted for or on behalf of foreign powers, organizations, or persons, or their agents, or international terrorist organizations or activities."

Under Executive Order 12333, several governmental agencies of the intelligence community have counterintelligence responsibilities, however, the Federal Bureau of Investigation has assumed the lead counterintelligence role. Accordingly and to meet its obligations under the order, the Bureau adopted the following goals:

- Protect the secrets of the U.S. Intelligence Community, using intelligence to focus investigative efforts, and collaborating with our government partners to reduce the risk of espionage and insider threats.

- Protect the nation's critical assets, like advanced technologies and sensitive information in the defense, intelligence, economic, financial, public health, and science and technology sectors.

- Counter the activities of foreign spies. Through proactive investigations, the Bureau identifies who they are and stops what they are doing.

- Keep weapons of mass destruction from falling into the wrong hands, and use intelligence to drive the FBI's investigative efforts to keep threats from becoming reality.

Notice as a preliminary matter that protecting the AI assets of the United States falls within the scope of those self-defined goals. And those goals are useful reference points for understanding the counterintelligence world. But let's dive in a bit deeper to set up a framework for comments I will make later about the AI-related counterintelligence threat. So here are 10 general points that I think are relevant to understanding the counterintelligence world:

Counterintelligence is reactive

Counterintelligence is about stopping bad things from happening. It is about identifying and countering the intelligence activities of hostile foreign intelligence services and other hostile foreign actors, such as terrorist organizations. This includes countering both clandestine intelligence gathering activities and other clandestine intelligence activities. The former category is what many might think of as traditional spying; the latter is more like conducting sabotage and secret influence and disinformation campaigns to manipulate a foreign population. Those "other" clandestine intelligence activities would fall within the category of what people in the United States would think of as "covert action"—activities seeking to influence political, economic or military conditions abroad, where it is intended that the role of the particular government is kept secret.

Counterintelligence is proactive

To be effective, counterintelligence must not be just reactive; it also must be aggressively proactive. So if you are a counterintelligence official, you are proactively trying to collect information about the identities of your adversaries; what they are thinking, planning and doing; and whom they have recruited, co-opted or fooled into help them. You have to be willing to take thoughtful and well-considered risks to recruit sources inside hostile foreign intelligence services and on foreign soil. You have to deploy sensitive technical collection techniques, tactics and procedures to spy on adversaries. All activities in this regard need to be intelligence-driven, strategic and executed using the best possible tradecraft.

Counterintelligence is protective

As a counterintelligence official, you are trying to protect and defend the nation, its people, its assets, and those of its allies from your adversaries. Indeed, the motto of the British Security Service or MI-5 as it is more widely known, which is Britain's lead counterintelligence agency, is "Regnum Defende" ("Defence of the Realm"). MI-5 says that its "mission is to keep the country safe. For more than a century, scientists have worked to protect people from danger whether it is from terrorism or damaging espionage by hostile states." You have to understand comprehensively and deeply what are the most important national assets to protect.

For example, you might need a comprehensive heat map of all the valuable assets of the entire nation; or of a particular geographic region or important sectors of the economy, telecommunications system or the defense industrial base that you need to protect. You might want a heat map of the AI ecosystem that catalogs what assets you need to protect, how vulnerable they are, how effectively the risks to those assets have been mitigated and what gaps remain. You also need to understand what the bad guys think they need to do regarding what you are trying to protect—in other words, what do they think they need to steal or corrupt? Unfortunately, you will never be certain about whether you or they have a better picture of what assets they should focus on.

Counterintelligence challenges are overwhelming

There are too many adversaries and too much to protect. In a free society, you cannot defend against everyone everywhere all the time. You have to prioritize the threats and what you are trying to protect; your heat map will help. Too often, the adversaries will win.

Counterintelligence is done at home

Counterintelligence activities occur mainly domestically, even though they are focused on hostile foreign intelligence services. Of course, adversaries operate globally, and they will try to recruit and exploit Americans abroad and will engage in malicious cyber activities anywhere, but mostly they focus on the U.S. homeland. This means that counterintelligence authorities must find foreign intelligence operatives who are hiding domestically and mixing in and interacting with the very people you are trying to protect. As a result, it is often hard to find the bad guys as well as the Americans who are helping them, either wittingly or unwittingly. This is the same type of problem counterterrorism officials face.

Because all of this is happening at home, counterintelligence activities intended to identify and disrupt intelligence threats domestically necessarily pose risks to the civil liberties of Americans. To be effective, counterintelligence officials must engage in a range of intrusive clandestine activities in the United States intended to thwart their adversaries, including electronic surveillance, surreptitious searches, recruitment of sources, physical surveillance, and undercover operations. Such activities undertaken here at home invariably implicate the rights of Americans no matter how hard counterintelligence officials try to avoid doing so.

Counterintelligence is confusing

Your adversary is actively trying to deceive you, and it is hard to figure out what is going on. It is easy to make mistakes—you can easily miss real threats, plots and actors, and you can waste time, resources and effort following the wrong people or countering the wrong or nonexistent plot. Your adversary is trying to get you to be complacent or chase your tail, and, if you are not careful, it is all too easy to let that happen.

Counterintelligence is sophisticated

Effective foreign intelligence services are very important for the security, political stability, and economic well-being of nations. Foreign intelligence collection provides national leaders and government agencies with the information they need to make informed military, diplomatic, economic, and other important decisions; anticipate and address the actions of foreign nations; and protect the nation from attack, sabotage, and other threatening activities by adversaries. As a result, countries are going to invest a lot in making sure that their intelligence services can defeat counterintelligence efforts to stop them.

Accordingly, foreign intelligence adversaries are well resourced, experienced, dedicated, motivated and aggressive. They use complex, novel and subtle means to defeat counterintelligence services. They recruit and place sources; they co-opt or threaten insiders; they conduct physical and electronic surveillance and break-ins; and they engage in sophisticated intelligence tradecraft to obscure their activities and deceive adversaries and innocent third parties. Moreover, the spy business has changed a great deal over the years with the advent of the Internet and the explosion of open-source information. And intelligence activities are now inextricably intertwined with the digital ecosystem, malicious cyber activities, and advanced perception management and manipulation campaigns.

The essence of the clandestine intelligence-gathering business (i.e., espionage) is to collect secret information by secret means. In other words: (a) someone wants to protect the information, data, technology, weapons systems or other important assets from being stolen, damaged or destroyed; (b) spies want to steal or do other bad things to those assets; and (c) the spies want to do so, if at all possible, in a way that keeps the victim from knowing or understanding what happened. From the spy's perspective, it is best if the victim never knows that something was stolen or corrupted or, if the victim does find out that something bad happened to the asset, that the victim does not know the identity or role of the spy in the activity.

U.S. counterintelligence officials must figure out how to deal with all of this. And while they have to adhere strictly to the Constitution and laws of the United States, their adversaries follow different rules or no rules at all. The same is true for your closest foreign partners, who must follow the rules of their own countries.

Some people have likened the counterterrorism challenge to that faced by a soccer team that cannot allow the opposing side to score even one goal. In both the counterterrorism and counterintelligence contexts the situation is actually much worse. Imagine that the soccer team not only needs to prevent the opposing team from scoring any goals but also has to deal with an opposing side that may be either invisible or wearing uniforms identical to their own; that plays by different rules or no rules at all; that can score by leaving the field and lifting up the net from behind and putting the ball in for a goal; and that all of this is happening on a field that is undulating and otherwise changing constantly because of the dynamic nature of technology, the economy, and the intelligence needs of adversaries. Counterintelligence is hard and requires sophistication, in part, because the environment can be highly disorienting.

For a variety of reasons, the field of counterintelligence has at times been considered a backwater by some and has played second fiddle to efforts to address ordinary crime before 9/11 and counterterrorism after 9/11. Counterintelligence investigations, however, present some of the most complex and vexing problems that a national security agency can face. For example, the counterintelligence investigations of Robert Hanssen, the Russian illegals network eventually known as "Ghost Stories", the Russian efforts to influence the 2016 presidential election, and a plethora of cyber-enabled foreign intelligence activities by China and others demonstrate the sophisticated nature of counterintelligence work. To appropriately disrupt the activities of foreign intelligence services while preserving the long-term efficacy of their sensitive sources and methods, counterintelligence officials are regularly called upon to make hard choices about whether, when and how to carry out such disruptions.

Counterintelligence is forever

Hostile foreign intelligence services represent persistent threats. Nation-state adversaries generally don't go away or give up, even if regimes change. For example, the FBI has been dealing with intelligence threats from the Soviet Union and the Russian Federation since 1917. The FBI will be dealing with the intelligence threat from China for as long as it exists. To be sure, the clandestine intelligence activities of foreign powers change over time depending upon the needs of the country and developments in fields such as science and technology, politics, and the economy. So, counterintelligence officials must be adaptive and creative over an extended period.

Counterintelligence is powerful

The FBI has all of its national security and law enforcement authorities available to use against hostile foreign intelligence services and their agents. It can leverage the resources of its partners in the U.S. intelligence community; other federal agencies; its foreign intelligence, counterintelligence, and law enforcement partners around the globe; and approximately 18,000 domestic law enforcement agencies. It has the authority and capability to conduct highly intrusive electronic surveillance and searches of Americans and others in the United States without ever being required to tell them that it did so. It can arrest Americans and others in the United States, and seek the arrest and extradition of anyone anywhere.

But as many casual observers do not understand, arrest and prosecution of foreign intelligence operatives are not the only ways to thwart the intelligence activities of hostile foreign adversaries. Without going into much detail here, counterintelligence officials have a range of other options available to identify, understand, and disrupt the activities of foreign powers and their agents. These include recruiting and doubling-back sources the adversaries themselves have recruited (i.e., "double agents"); deporting foreign nationals with the help of the Department of Homeland Security and kicking foreign diplomats out of the country with the help of the State Department; providing information to support diplomatic actions or the imposition of economic sanctions; public exposure; and providing defensive briefings to individuals or organizations that are being targeted by a hostile service. Counterintelligence officials can accomplish their mission even if no one is ever prosecuted or jailed, and they will continue their mission even if there is no prospect of arrests and prosecutions.

Combined with the forever nature of counterintelligence, this point has important implications. There is a constant spy-vs.-spy quality to counterintelligence: us watching them, and them watching us. It has a plethora of different modalities. And it never stops.

Counterintelligence is highly regulated

Because of the nature and scope of the counterintelligence activities described above, and the misuse of counterintelligence authorities and resources in the past against Americans such as with the FBI's investigation of Dr. Martin Luther King Jr. in the 1960s, counterintelligence activities are highly regulated in the United States. For example, the FBI must conduct its counterintelligence activities in conformance with Attorney General Guidelines, the Foreign Intelligence Surveillance Act (FISA) and a range of other federal statutes that regulate its actions. The FBI is accountable with respect to its counterintelligence mission to the attorney general, the director of national intelligence, the inspectors general of the Department of Justice and the U.S. intelligence community, and the permanent intelligence committees of Congress. In a free society, it is essential to have robust oversight and accountability mechanisms in place to monitor the activities of all counterintelligence agencies.

Overriding catastrophic and existential threat

Major personalities like Stephen Hawking, Bill Gates, and Elon Musk have spoken loudly about the hypothetical existential threat brought about by the possible advent of super intelligence.

If these machines can learn by themselves and even mutate their own algorithms without human input, what is to stop them from mutating into an intelligence far more advanced that the human that created them? What is to stop this super intelligence from laying waste to the human race and superimpose itself as the new emperor?

Dangerous AI

AI in its current form is mostly harmless, but that's not going to last. Machines are getting smarter and more capable by the minute, leading to concerns that AI will eventually match, and then exceed, human levels of intelligence a prospect known as artificial superintelligence (ASI).

As a technological prospect, ASI will be unlike anything you've ever encountered before. ASI operators have no prior experience to guide them, which means they're going to have to put their collective heads together and start preparing. It's not hyperbole to say humanity's existence is at stake—as hard as that is to hear and admit—and given there's no consensus on when you can expect to meet your new digital overlords, it would be incumbent upon us to start preparing now for this possibility, and not wait until some arbitrary date in the future.

On the horizon

Indeed, the return of an AI winter, a period in which innovations in AI slow down appreciably, no longer seems likely. Fueled primarily by the powers of machine learning, we've entered into a golden era of AI research, and with no apparent end in sight. In recent years we've witnessed startling progress in areas such as independent learning, foresight, autonomous navigation, computer vision, and video gameplay. Computers can now trade stocks in the order of milliseconds, automated cars are increasingly appearing on your streets, and artificially intelligent assistants have encroached into your homes. The coming years will bear witness to further advances, including AI that can learn through its own experiences, adapt to novel situations, and comprehend abstractions and analogies.

By definition, ASI will understand the world and humans better than we understand it, and it's not obvious at all how we could control something like that. Nobody knows when ASI will arise or what form it will take, but the signs of its impending arrival are starting to appear.

Last year, for example, in a bot-on-bot Go tournament, DeepMind's AlphaGo Zero (AGZ) defeated the regular AlphaGo by a score of 100 games to zero. Incredibly, AGZ required just three days training itself from scratch, during which time it acquired thousands of years of human Go playing experience. As the DeepMind researchers noted, it is now "possible to train [machines] to superhuman level, without human examples or guidance, given no knowledge of the domain beyond basic rules." It was a stark reminder that developments in this field are susceptible to rapid, unpredictable, and dramatic improvements, and that we've entered into a new era—the age of superintelligent machines.

"According to several estimates, supercomputers can now—or in the near future—do more elementary operations per second than human brains, so we might already have the necessary hardware to compete with brains," said Jaan Tallinn, a computer programmer, founding member of Skype, and co-founder of the Centre for the Study of Existential Risk, a research center at the University of Cambridge concerned with human extinction scenarios. "Also, a lot of research effort is now going into 'meta learning'—that is, developing AIs that would be able to design AIs. Therefore, progress in AI might at some point simply decouple from human speeds and timelines."

These and other developments will likely lead to the introduction of AGI, otherwise known as artificial general intelligence. Unlike ANI, artificial narrow intelligence or narrow AI, which is super good at solving specialized tasks, like playing Go or recognizing human faces, AGI will exhibit proficiency across multiple domains. This powerful form of AI will be more humanlike in its abilities, adapting to new situations, learning a wide variety of skills, and performing an extensive variety of tasks. Once AGI is achieved, the step to superintelligence will be a short one—especially if AGIs are told to create increasingly better versions of them.

"It is difficult to predict technological advancement, but a few factors indicate that AGI and ASI might be possible within the next several decades," said Yolanda Lannquist, AI policy researcher at The Future Society, a non-profit think tank concerned with the impacts of emerging technologies. She points to companies currently working towards AGI development, including Google DeepMind, GoodAI, Araya Inc., Vicarious, SingularityNET, among others, including smaller teams and individuals at universities. At the same time, Lannquist said research on ANI may lead to breakthroughs towards AGI, with companies such as Facebook, Google, IBM, Microsoft, Amazon, Apple, OpenAI, Tencent, Baidu, and Xiaomi among the major companies currently investing heavily in AI research.

With AI increasingly entering into our lives, we are starting to see unique problems emerge, particularly in areas of privacy, security, and fairness. AI ethics boards are starting to become commonplace, for example, along with standards projects to ensure safe and ethical machine intelligence. Looking ahead, we're going to have to deal with such developments as massive technological unemployment, the rise of autonomous killing machines including weaponized drones, AI-enabled hacking, and other threats.

Beyond levels of comprehension and control

But these are problems of the present and the near future, and most of us can agree that measures should be taken to mitigate these negative aspects of AI. More controversially, however, is the suggestion that we begin preparing for the advent of artificial superintelligence; that heralded moment when machines will eventually surpass human levels of intelligence by several orders of magnitude. What makes ASI particularly dangerous is that it will operate beyond human levels of control and cognitive capacity. Owing to its tremendous reach, speed, and computational proficiency, ASI will be capable of accomplishing virtually anything it's programmed or decides to do.

"Conjuring ASI-inspired doomsday scenarios is actually quite beside the point; we already have it within our means to destroy ourselves."

Whilst there are many extreme scenarios that come to mind, an ASI could destroy our civilization, either by accident, misintention, or deliberate design. For instance, it could turn our planet into goo after a simple misunderstanding of its goals (the allegorical paperclip scenario is a good example), remove humanity as a troublesome nuisance, or wipe out civilization and infrastructure as it strives to improve itself even further, a possibility AI theorists refer to as recursive self-improvement. Should humanity embark upon an AI arms race with rival nations, a weaponized ASI could get out of control, either during peacetime or during war. An ASI could intentionally end humanity by destroying our planet's atmosphere or biosphere with self-replicating nanotechnology. Or it could launch all nuclear weapons, spark a Terminator-style robopocalypse, or unleash some powers of physics we do not even know about. Using genetics, cybernetics, nanotechnology, or other means at its disposal, an ASI could reengineer us into blathering, mindless automatons, thinking it was doing us some sort of favor in an attempt to pacify our violent natures. Rival ASIs could wage war against themselves in a battle for resources, scorching the planet in the process.

Clearly, we have no shortage of ideas, but conjuring ASI-inspired doomsday scenarios is actually quite beside the point; we already have it within our means to destroy ourselves, and it will not be difficult for ASI to come up with its own ways to end humanity. This scenario, admittedly being capable of being a science fiction movie, has nonetheless been a matter of concern for a growing number of prominent thinkers and concerned citizens alike who have started to further the matter and to carefully adjust their views accordingly. Tallinn said once ASI emerges, it'll confront us with entirely new types of problems. "By definition, ASI will understand the world and humans better than we understand it, and it's not obvious at all how we could control something like that," said Tallinn. "If you think about it, what happens to chimpanzees is no longer up to them, because we humans control their environment by being more intelligent. We should work on AI alignment to avoid a similar fate."

Katja Grace, editor of the AI Impacts blog and a researcher at the Machine Intelligence Research Institute (MIRI), said ASI will be the first technology to potentially surpass humans on every dimension. "So far, humans have had a monopoly on decision-making, and therefore had control over everything," she told Gizmodo. "With AI, this may end."

Stuart Russell, a professor of computer science and an expert in AI at the University of California, Berkeley, said humans should be concerned about the potential for ASI for one simple reason: intelligence is power.

"Evolution and history do not provide good examples of a less powerful class of entities retaining power indefinitely over a more powerful class of entities," Russell told Gizmodo. "We do not yet know how to control ASI, because, traditionally, control over other entities seems to require the ability to out-think and out-anticipate—and, by definition, we cannot out-think and out-anticipate ASI. We have to take an approach to designing AI systems that somehow sidesteps this basic problem."

Be prepared

Okay, so we have our work cut out for ourselves. But we shouldn't despair, or worse, do nothing—there are things we can do in the here-and-now. Nick Bostrom, author of Superintelligence: Paths, Dangers, Strategies and a philosopher at Oxford's Future of Humanity Institute, said no specific protocols or sweeping changes to society are required today, but he agreed to do consequential research in this area.

"A few years ago the argument that we should do nothing may have made sense, as we had no real idea on how we should research this and make meaningful progress," Bostrom told Gizmodo. "But concepts and ideas are now in place, and we can break it down into chunks worthy of research." He said this could take the form of research papers, think tanks, seminars, and so on. "People are now doing important research work in this area," said Bostrom, "It's something we can hammer away at and make incremental progress."

Russell agreed, saying humans should think about ways of developing and designing AI systems that are safe and beneficial, regardless of how intelligent the components become. He believes this is possible, provided the components are defined, trained, and connected in the right way.

Indeed, this is something you should be doing already. Prior to the advent of AGI and ASI, we'll have to contend with the threats posed by more basic, narrow AI—the kind that's already starting to appear in the infrastructure. By solving the problems posed by current AI, you could learn some valuable lessons and set some important precedents that could pave the way to building safe, but even more powerful AI, in the future.

Take the prospect of autonomous vehicles, for example. Once deployed en masse, self-driving cars will be monitored, and to a certain extent controlled, by a central intelligence. This overseeing "brain" will send software updates to its fleet, advise cars on traffic conditions, and serve as the overarching network's communication hub. But imagine if someone were to hack into this system and send malicious instructions to the fleet. It would be a disaster on an epic scale. Such is the threat of AI.

"Cybersecurity of AI systems is a major hole," Lannquist told Gizmodo. "Autonomous systems, such as autonomous vehicles, personal assistant robots, AI toys, drones, and even weaponized systems are subject to cyber attacks and hacking, to spy, steal, delete or alter information or data, halt or disrupt service, and even hijacking," she said. "Meanwhile, there is a talent shortage in cybersecurity among governments and companies."

Another major risk, according to Lannquist, is bias in the data sets used to train machine learning algorithms. The resulting models aren't fit for everyone, she said, leading to problems of inclusion, equality, fairness, and even the potential for physical harm. An autonomous vehicle or surgical robot may not be sufficiently trained on enough images to discern humans of different skin color or sizes, for example. Scale this up to the level of ASI, and the problem becomes exponentially worse.

Commercial face recognition software, for example, has repeatedly been shown to be less accurate on people with darker skin. Meanwhile, a predictive policing algorithm called PredPol was shown to unfairly target certain neighborhoods. And in a truly disturbing case, the COMPAS algorithm, which predicts the likelihood of recidivism to guide sentencing, was found to be racially biased. This is happening today—imagine the havoc and harm an ASI could inflict with greater power, scope, and social reach.

It will also be important for humans to stay within the comprehension loop, meaning people need to maintain an understanding of an AI's decision making rationale. This is already proving to be difficult as AI keeps encroaching into superhuman realms. This is what's known as the "black box" problem, and it happens when developers are at a loss to explain the behavior of their creations. Making something safe when you don't have full understanding of how it works is a precarious proposition at best. Accordingly, efforts will be required to create AIs that are capable of explaining themselves in ways we puny humans can comprehend.

Thankfully, that's already happening. Last year, for example, DARPA gave $6.5 million to computer scientists at Oregon State University to address this issue. The four-year grant will support the development of new methodologies designed to help researchers make better sense of the digital gobbledygook inside black boxes, most notably by getting AIs to explain to humans why they reached certain decisions, or what their conclusions actually mean.

We also need to change the corporate culture around the development of AI, particularly in Silicon Valley where the prevailing attitude is to "fail hard and fast or die slow." This sort of mentality won't work for strong AI, which will require extreme caution, consideration, and foresight. Cutting corners and releasing poorly thought out systems could end in disaster.

"Through more collaboration, such as AGI researchers pooling their resources to form a consortia, industry-led guidelines and standards, or technical standards and norms, we can hopefully re-engineer this 'race to the bottom' in safety standards, and instead have a 'race to the top,'" said Lannquist. "In a 'race to the top,' companies take time to uphold ethical and safety standards. Meanwhile, the competition is beneficial because it can speed up progress towards beneficial innovation, like AI for UN Sustainable Development Goals."

At the same time, corporations should consider information sharing, particularly if a research lab has stumbled upon a particularly nasty vulnerability, like an algorithm that can sneak past encryption schemes, spread to domains outside an intended realm, or be easily weaponized.

Changing corporate culture won't be easy, but it needs to start at the top. To facilitate this, companies should create a new executive position, a Chief Safety Officer (CSO), or something similar, to oversee the development of what could be catastrophically dangerous AI, among other dangerous emerging technologies.

Governments and other public institutions have a role to play as well. Russell said we need well-informed groups, committees, agencies, and other institutions within governments that have access to top-level AI researchers. We also need to develop standards for safe AI system design, he added.

"Governments can incentivize research for AI safety, through grants, awards, and grand challenges," added Lannquist. "The private sector or academia can contribute or collaborate on research with AI safety organizations. AI researchers can organize to uphold ethical and safe AI development procedures, and research organizations can set up processes for whistle-blowing."

Action is also required at the international level. The existential dangers posed by AI are potentially more severe than climate change, yet there is still no equivalent to the International Panel for Climate Change (IPCC). How about an International Panel for AI? In addition, to establishing and enforcing standards and regulations, this panel could serve as a "safe space" for AI developers who believe they're working on something particularly dangerous. A good rule of thumb would be to stop development, and seek council with this panel. On a similar note, and as some previous developments in biotechnology have shown, some research findings are too dangerous to share with the general public (e.g. "gain-of-function" studies in which viruses are deliberately mutated to infect humans). An international AI panel could decide which technological breakthroughs should stay secret for reasons of international security. Conversely, as per the rationale of the gain-of-function studies, the open sharing of knowledge could result in the development of proactive safety measures. Given the existential nature of ASI, however, it's tough to imagine the ingredients of our doom being passed around for all to see. This will be a tricky area to navigate.

On a more general level, there is need to get more people working on the problem, including mathematicians, logicians, ethicists, economists, social scientists, and philosophers.

A number of groups have already started to address the ASI problem, including Oxford's Future of Humanity Institute, MIRI, the UC Berkeley Center for Human-Compatible AI, OpenAI, and Google Brain. Other initiatives include the Asilomar Conference, which has already established guidelines for the safe development of AI, and the Open Letter on AI signed by many prominent thinkers, including the late physicist Stephen Hawking, Tesla and SpaceX founder Elon Musk, and others.

Russell said the general public can contribute as well—but they need to educate themselves about the issues.

"Learn about some of the new ideas and read some of the technical papers, not just media articles about Musk—Zuckerberg smackdowns," he said. "Think about how those ideas apply to your work. For example, if you work on visual classification, what objective is the algorithm optimizing? What is the loss matrix? Are you sure that misclassifying a cat as a dog has the same cost as misclassifying a human as a gorilla? If not, think about how to do classification learning with an uncertain loss matrix."

Ultimately, Russell said it is important to avoid a tribalist mindset.

"Don't imagine that a discussion of risk is 'anti-AI.' It's not. It's a complement to AI. It's saying, "AI has the potential to impact the world," he said. "Just as biology has grown up and physics has grown up and accepted some responsibility for its impact on the world, it's time for AI to grow up—unless, that is, you really believe that AI will never have any impact and will never work."

The ASI problem is poised to be the most daunting challenge this generation species has ever faced, and we very well may fail. But we have to try.

The deployment challenge

We have an interest in embracing AI, given its likely contributions to business value, economic growth, and social good, at a time when many economies need to boost productivity. Businesses and countries have a strong incentive to keep up with global leaders such as the United States and China. Increased and broad deployment will require accelerating the progress being made on the technical challenges, as well making sure that all potential users have access to AI and can benefit from it. Among measures that may be needed:

- Investing in and continuing to advance AI research and innovation in a manner that ensures that the benefits can be shared by all.

- Expanding available data sets, especially in areas where their use would drive wider benefits for the economy and society.

- Investing in AI-relevant human capital and infrastructure to broaden the talent base capable of creating and executing AI solutions to keep pace with global AI leaders.

- Encouraging increased AI literacy among business leaders and policy makers to guide informed decision making.

- Supporting existing digitization efforts that form the foundation for eventual AI deployment for both organizations and countries.

The responsible AI challenge

AI will not live up to its promise if the public loses confidence in it as a result of privacy violations, bias, or malicious use, or if much of the world comes to blame it for exacerbating inequality. Establishing confidence in its abilities to do good, at the same time as addressing misuses, will be critical. Approaches could include:

- Strengthening consumer, data, and privacy and security protections.

- Establishing a generally shared framework and set of principles for the beneficial and safe use of AI.

- Best practice sharing and ongoing innovation to address issues such as safety, bias, and explainability.

- Striking the right balance between the business and national competitive race to lead in AI to ensure that the benefits of AI are widely available and shared.

CHAPTER 10
ETHICS IN MACHINE LEARNING

Imagine, in the near future, a bank using a machine learning algorithm to recommend mortgage applications for approval. A rejected applicant brings a lawsuit against the bank, alleging that the algorithm is discriminating racially against mortgage applicants. The bank replies that this is impossible, since the algorithm is deliberately blinded to the race of the applicants. Indeed, that was part of the bank's rationale for implementing the system. Even so, statistics show that the bank's approval rate for black applicants has been steadily dropping. Submitting ten apparently equally qualified genuine applicants as determined by a separate panel of human judges shows that the algorithm accepts white applicants and rejects black applicants. What could possibly be happening?

Finding an answer may not be easy. If the machine learning algorithm is based on a complicated neural network or a genetic algorithm produced by directed evolution, then it may prove nearly impossible to understand why, or even how, the algorithm is judging applicants based on their race. On the other hand, a machine learner based on decision trees or Bayesian networks is much more transparent to programmer inspection, which may enable an auditor to discover that the AI algorithm uses the address information of applicants who were born or previously resided in predominantly poverty-stricken areas.

AI algorithms play an increasingly large role in modern society, though usually not labeled "AI." The scenario described above might be transpiring even as I write. It will become increasingly important to develop AI algorithms that are not just powerful and scalable, but also transparent to inspection—to name one of many socially important properties.

Some challenges of machine ethics are much like many other challenges involved in designing machines. Designing a robot arm to avoid crushing stray humans is no more morally fraught than designing a flame-retardant sofa. It involves new programming challenges, but no new ethical challenges. But when AI algorithms take on cognitive work with social dimensions-cognitive tasks previously performed by humans—the AI algorithm inherits the social requirements. It would surely be frustrating to find that no bank in the world will approve your seemingly excellent loan application, and nobody knows why, and nobody can find out even in principle. Maybe you have a first name strongly associated with deadbeats? Who knows?

Transparency is not the only desirable feature of AI. It is also important that AI algorithms taking over social functions be predictable to those they govern. To understand the importance of such predictability, consider an analogy. The legal principle of stare decisions binds judges to follow past precedent whenever possible. To an engineer, this preference for precedent may seem incomprehensible—why bind the future to the past, when technology is always improving? But one of the most important functions of the legal system is to be predictable, so that, e.g., contracts can be written knowing how they will be executed. The job of the legal system is not necessarily to optimize society, but to provide a predictable environment within which citizens can optimize their own lives.

It will also become increasingly important that AI algorithms be robust against manipulation. A machine vision system to scan airline luggage for bombs must be robust against human adversaries deliberately searching for exploitable flaws in the algorithm—for example, a shape that, placed next to a pistol in one's luggage, would neutralize recognition of it. Robustness against manipulation is an ordinary criterion in information security; nearly *the* criterion. But it is not a criterion that appears often in machine learning journals, which are currently more interested in, e.g., how an algorithm scales up on larger parallel systems.

Another important social criterion for dealing with organizations is being able to find the person responsible for getting something done. When an AI system fails at its assigned task, who takes the blame? The programmers? The end-users? Modern bureaucrats often take refuge in established procedures that distribute responsibility so widely that no one person can be identified to blame for the catastrophes that result. The provably disinterested judgment of an expert system could turn out to be an even better refuge. Even if an AI system is designed with a user override, one must consider the career incentive of a bureaucrat who will be personally blamed if the override goes wrong, and who would much prefer to blame the AI for any difficult decision with a negative outcome.

Responsibility, transparency, auditability, incorruptibility, predictability, and a tendency to not make innocent victims scream with helpless frustration: all criteria that apply to humans performing social functions; all criteria that must be considered in an algorithm intended to replace human judgment of social functions; all criteria that may not appear in a journal of machine learning considering how an algorithm scales up to more computers. This list of criteria is by no means exhaustive, but it serves as a small sample of what an increasingly computerized society should be thinking about.

CHAPTER 11

WHY REGULATING AI COULD BE DIFFICULT

New technologies often spur public anxiety, but the intensity of concern about the implications of advances in AI is particularly noteworthy. Several respected scholars and technology leaders warn that AI is on the path to turning robots into a master class that will subjugate humanity if not destroy it. Others fears that AI is enabling governments to mass-produce autonomous weapons— "killing machines"—that will choose their own targets, including innocent civilians. Renowned economists point out that AI, unlike previous technologies, is destroying many more jobs than it creates, leading to major economic disruptions.

There seems to be widespread agreement that AI growth is accelerating. After waves of hype followed by disappointment, computers have now defeated chess, Jeopardy, Go, and poker champions. Policymakers and the public are impressed by driverless cars that have already traveled several million miles. Calls from scholars and public intellectuals for imposing government regulations on AI research and development (R&D) are gaining traction. Although AI developments undoubtedly deserve attention, humans must be careful to avoid applying too broad a brush. We agree with the findings of a study panel organized as part of Stanford University's One Hundred Year Study of AI: "The Study Panel's consensus is that attempts to regulate 'AI' in general would be misguided, since there is no clear definition of AI (it isn't any one thing), and the risks and considerations are very different in different domains."

Developing AI systems is not an easy process. AI technologies are diverse and can be developed by people operating in different countries with different skill sets, posing the challenge of discreet advancement.

Moreover, because of self-learning, most AI systems may operate in ways that the original programmers did not anticipate, creating issues with programmable foreseeability and general control.

It can be hard to detect and therefore control AI projects due to latent opacity and lack of regulatory and jurisprudential preparedness.

Regulation is mostly effective when formulated on the face of hard factual evidence of the consequences of the object under consideration. Yet, with AI, there is largely no empirical knowledge of the issues that will arise with the widespread adoption of the technologies because of their diversity, novelty, and unpredictability.

Finally, there is a definition problem with AI. Just what is AI? Regulation is impossible without proper, binding and permanent definition of the object under consideration, and AI is very diverse and always changing in form and purpose.

Should the government regulate AI?

As nearly every day brings additional news about how AI will affect the way we live, a heated debate has broken out over what the United States should do about it. On the one hand, the likes of Elon Musk and Stephen Hawking argue that human must regulate now to slow down and develop general principles governing AI's development because of its potential to cause massive economic dislocation and even destroy human civilization.

On the other hand, AI advocates argue that there is no consensus on what AI is, let alone what it can ultimately do. Regulating AI in such circumstances, these advocates claim, will simply stifle innovation and cede to other countries the technological initiative that has done so much to power the U.S. economy.

However, the intense focus on these foundational questions threatens to obscure a key point: AI is already subject to regulation in many ways, and, even while the broader debates about AI continue, additional regulations look sure to follow. These regulations aren't the sort of broad principles that Musk and Hawking urge and AI advocates fear: There's nothing on the books as dramatic "a robot may not injure a human being or, through inaction, allow a human being to come to harm." This is the first of Isaac Asimov's famed three laws of robotics.

Thus far, most of the rules aren't particular to AI at all. Rather, they are existing and sometimes longstanding privacy, cybersecurity, unfair and deceptive trade acts and practices, due process, and health and safety rules that cover technologies that now happen to be considered "AI." These include rules about holding, using and protecting personal data, guidance on how to manage the risks caused by financial algorithms, and protections against discrimination.

To be sure, many of these rules are of the subjects of intense debate over, for example, whether they sufficiently protect consumers. The application of these existing legal frameworks and regulatory schemes to AI technologies can present difficult questions. For example, how do human-centric concepts like intent apply to robots? But even the more recent enactments that do specifically address AI, such as the many state laws governing autonomous vehicles, shy away from making general pronouncements about AI technology, instead choosing to target particular risks caused by specific applications.

This also seems to be the direction in which Congress is headed. As AI has taken off, Capitol Hill has largely held back, at least until the second half of 2017, when members introduced three separate pieces of AI-related legislation: the House-passed the Self Drive Act, which addresses the safety of automated vehicles, the AV Start Act, a bipartisan Senate companion that similarly tackles driverless cars, and the Future of AI Act, a bipartisan Senate bill that would create an advisory committee on AI issues.

While all of these bills acknowledge the potential dislocations that animate Musk and Hawking's concerns, they shy away from broad pronouncements about AI generally in favor of further study and a focus on addressing sector-specific questions as they arise. Indeed, the most general bill, the Future of AI Act, would merely establish a generalist body to study and provide advice on AI issues.

Conversely, the other two bills feature the statutory provisions with immediate impact through the preemption of certain state laws to ensure that the path is clear for innovation without the complications caused by disparate state regulatory regimes. These bills, the ones with actual bite, focus exclusively on the sector where states have begun to take an active role and where technology is already poised to have a near-term and real-world impact, which is automated vehicle technology.

It is tempting to look at these developments and conclude that industry and innovators would be safe in continuing to comply with the laws that affect them today while waiting to see what Congress does if and when it decides to focus on the particular type of AI technology that they are developing, in other words, when their sector is under the legislative gun, as autonomous vehicle technology is today. But such an approach would be misguided.

The consideration of the bills in Congress discussed above shows that legislators are seized of the many issues presented by the rapid development of AI technology. While Congress is taking incremental steps for the time being, the processes these bills set in motion could have long-term impacts. Even if these bills don't immediately or directly affect a company's sector, they could still have path setting effects.

Decisions made today may have substantial ripple effects that legislators could easily miss on the development of AI technology down the road. Who could have possibly imagined the full implications of Section 230 of the Communications Decency Act when it was enacted in 1996? Or the effect of the Electronic Communication Privacy Act's warrant requirement for emails less than 180 days old in 1986? Early legislative enactments about new technologies tend to persist.

The very vocabulary that regulators are beginning to use in these bills could have a lasting impact on the way that regulators view and treat AI technologies more generally. If companies don't, for example, establish an AI lexicon that will help legislators or regulators understand, meaningfully describe, and distinguish between technologies that should be regulated differently, those legislators and regulators may very well develop such a lexicon themselves. Likewise, if companies don't make legislators or regulators aware of their industry best practices and model policies or codes of conduct, there's no chance those can serve as a guide as legislators look for models that work.

To the extent that existing legal regimes are affecting AI innovations and the frameworks within which they are being developed, there is no time better than the present for bringing to the attention of regulators the ways those existing frameworks are or are not working. The AI regulatory agenda may be set early. The AI community should take notice. Regulation is not just to come. It is already here.

CHAPTER 12

AI TECHNOLOGIES AND THEIR USE CASES

The AI promise

Put simply, AI is being used to create machines that can;

Feel; Machines that can employ different AI technologies to replicate the complicated human psychological emotions in what is now known as affective computing.

Deduce: aka make decisions. Conclude. This is one of the primary uses of AI. It is a capability that is built into materials to decide on a result after analysing the parameters.

Recognize: Positive identification of features is important in AI applications. It allows for machines to make deductions, and execute outcomes.

Learn: The ability for machines to learn is probably one of the great innovations of AI. It allows machines to continually improve their 'current level of awareness.' With an increase in authentic data, machines will use algorithms that 'learn' and 'recall' better than humans.

Plan: Traditional corporate planning is hugely archaic and unresponsive to organic changes in the competitive and ever changing business environments.

Concepts like 'connected planning' can allow organizations to employ machine learning in removing planning deficiencies associated with human reasoning and knowledge silos by studying corporate data and accentuating market response for better results.

Execute: Decision Making is one of the ultimate goals of AI. We all want machines that can execute varied outcomes based on an accurate decision.

Such outcomes as prescribing medicine, robotic responses like self-driving cars and precision surgery are results of this AI functionality.

In short, people are just scratching the surface when it comes to the wider benefits brought about by the use of AI.

A combination of different AI technologies has been at the core of the development of various recent and quite prominent use cases.

AI manifests in several interrelated disciplines, including Neural Networks, Machine Learning, Natural Language Processing, Facial Recognition, Augmented Reality, Big Data Analytics, Robotics, Fuzzy Logic, Genetic algorithms, and Deep Learning.

It can impact virtually any business. The use cases can be for individuals, corporates or even governmental.

And they are many, so we are going to look at only three of the main areas where this technology impacts on the general public;

Healthcare

The most common use of AI in healthcare is through robots that primarily assist human medical staff by conducting mundane repetitive tasks and exponentially increase the safety and accuracy of medical processes.

Robots are now assisting surgeons reduce the time and errors associated with surgeries. Doctors can make very small incisions and using specialized robots carry out very invasive surgeries.

How are robots changing healthcare?

Robots are everywhere from science fiction to your local hospital, where they are changing healthcare. For the most part, these robots resemble R2D2 from Star Wars more than they do a humanoid, but they are making a big impact on the field of medicine. Robots in medicine help by relieving medical personnel from routine tasks, that take their time away from more pressing responsibilities, and by making medical procedures safer and less costly for patients. They can also perform accurate surgery in tiny places and transport dangerous substances.

Robots you already know

Robotic medical assistants monitor patient vital statistics and alert the nurses when there is a need for a human presence in the room, allowing nurses to monitor several patients at once. These robotic assistants also automatically enter information into the patient electronic health record. Robotic carts may be seen moving through hospital corridors carrying supplies. Robots are also assisting in surgery, allowing doctors to conduct surgery through as tiny incision instead of an inches-long incision. Robotics is making a big impact in other areas of medicine, as well.

New technology

Robotic technologies appear in many areas that directly affect patient care. They can be used to disinfect patient rooms and operating suites, reducing risks for patients, and medical personnel. They work in laboratories to take samples and then transport, analyze, and store them. This is especially good news if you have ever had blood drawn by someone who had to try several times to find a "good vein." The robotic lab assistant can locate that vessel and draw the blood with less pain and anxiety for the patient. Robots also prepare and dispense medications in pharmacological labs. In larger facilities robotic carts carry bed linens and even meals from floor to floor, riding elevators and maneuvering through automatic doors. There are also "gears and wires" robotic assistants that help paraplegics move and can administer physical therapy.

Robotic personal assistants can be built to look friendly and the Japanese have taken the lead on this front. One of their machines, called

Paro, responds to human speech and looks like a decidedly non-threatening baby seal. Other robotic technology is humanoid and used for help with personal care, socialization, and for training. One used in training emergency personnel to respond to trauma, for instance, looks like a victim who screams, bleeds and even responds to treatment.

Replacing human workers

The ultimate question for robotics in healthcare is whether they will take jobs away from humans. There are several reasons why the machines will not replace their human counterparts. For one thing, most hospitals have less than 300 beds. They simply cannot afford the technology. The automated guided vehicles require a dedicated hall or floor tracks and the installation of navigation devices throughout the facilities. Other carts work with the help of a laser-drawn map of the hospital programmed into them that includes elevators, turns and automated doors. That process is also extremely expensive. But ultimately, robotic assistants cannot replace basic human contact.

Even though the technology is expensive and some of it is years from being implemented, the use of robots is changing healthcare and — in ways you can only imagine— will continue to do so.

Here are some of the other very innovative uses that are being used for preventive and early-detection diagnosis of the major medical world killers.

Breast cancer detection using deep learning

Breast cancer is the most significant form of cancer for women. Breast cancer has the second highest mortality rate in women next to lung cancer. As per clinical statistics, 1 in every 8 women is diagnosed with breast cancer in their lifetime. However, periodic clinical checkups and self-tests help in early detection and thereby significantly increase the chances of survival. Invasive detection techniques cause rupture of the tumor, accelerating the spread of cancer to adjoining areas. Hence, there arises the need for a more robust, fast, accurate, and efficient noninvasive cancer detection system. In this work, an automated system is proposed for achieving error-free detection of breast cancer using mammogram. In this system, the deep learning techniques such as convolutional neural network, sparse autoencoder, and stacked sparse autoencoder are used. The performance of these techniques is analyzed and compared with the existing methods. From the analysis, it is observed that the stacked sparse autoencoder performs better compared to other methods. It also occurs in a small percentage of men.

Close to 270,000 women will be diagnosed with invasive breast cancer in the US in 2018, with another 64,000 having in situ breast cancer. More than 12% of all women in the US will develop breast cancer in any of the two forms in their lifetimes.

Early detection is therefore important to assist a reduction in mortality.

Deep learning can utilize historical data including billions of mammogram images to create algorithms that can diagnose malignant or chronic tumours at supersonic speeds with a high degree of accuracy.

Coupled with proper diagnosis, this will also eliminate the need for radiologists to carry out expensive and time consuming CAD confirmation tests before treating breast cancer.

These deep learning methods will benefit from worldwide networks that present as much data as can be uploaded from existing permitted databases.

Since the majority of biopsies find normal and benign results, most of the manual labeling of these microscopic images is redundant. Several existing machine learning approaches perform two-class (malignant, benign) and three-class (normal, in situ, invasive) classification through extraction of nuclei-related information. Benign lesions lack the ability to invade neighbors, so they are non-malignant. In-situ and invasive carcinoma, however, can spread to other areas, and therefore are malignant. Invasive tissues, unlike in-situ, can reach the surrounding normal tissues beyond the mammary ductal-lobular system.

Death rate due to breast cancer is very high. According to WHO (World health Organization) breast cancer impact over 1.5 million women each year worldwide. In 2015, 570,000 women died due to breast cancer which is approximately 15% of all deaths among women from cancer. In 2017 about 252,710 cases of breast cancer are diagnosed and about 40,610 women die in America.

Pakistan is at an alarming rate in Asia with 90,000 cases of breast cancer being booked annually, and death rate is approximately 40,000 per year. Death rate due to breast cancer can be reduced by following proper screening and diagnosis techniques at an initial stage before major physical symptoms start appearing on the body. Various techniques have been used for the detection of breast cancer by using ANN, support vector machine (SVM) etc. Mammography is a very effective and the most commonly used technique for the early detection of breast cancer. It even detects a very small change in the body.

Medical experts examine mammograms and recommend a biopsy if abnormalities are found in the mammogram. Biopsy is a standard clinical approach used to detect breast cancer, it is a costly, time-consuming, as well as painful procedure. Radiologist recommendation is very important at this stage, if it is a wrong diagnosis the patient has to go through an unnecessary biopsy.

Automation of this analysis helps radiologist to improve his diagnostic accuracy, such a type of system can be used as a second reader. A CAD system is proposed which helps to classify mammogram into one of its appropriate class i.e., benign (not harmful for the body and does not spread to other part of the body) or malignant (cell spreads to other part of the body and cause death).

Algorithms

To achieve a correct classification, the conventional method is often composed of three main steps: feature extraction, feature selection, and classification. These three steps need to be well-addressed separately and then integrated together. Extraction of discriminative features could potentially ease the latter steps of feature selection and classification. Nevertheless, the engineering of effective features is problem-oriented and highly depends on the quality of each intermediate result in the image processing, which often needs many passes of trial-and-error design and case-by-case user interventions.

The recent advances in deep learning technology can potentially change the design paradigm of image classification. Nature recently reported a work on classification of skin cancer using deep convolutional neural networks, which demonstrated a level of competence comparable to dermatologists. When scientists speak of "deep" learning, they are not simply referring to the number of layers. While there is no concrete definition of what "deep" means, it is the number of possible causal connections each neuron has that shapes the "depth" of deep learning structures.

Deep learning can directly uncover features from the training data without the explicit elaboration on feature extraction and selection. Neural networks operate by passing the input information through layers of neurons that transform the input information into the output. With the help of back propagation, the internal weights of neural networks get updated automatically based on the error information obtained from each iteration.

Diabetes onset detection using machine learning

Companies like DZone have developed diagnostic ensembles that combine to replicate positive identification of diabetes in an individual with a high success rate.

With good regulation, diabetes screening can be automated and made mandatory so that treatment can begin at onset.

Machine learning algorithms can help us to detect the onset of diabetes. Early detection of diabetes can reduce patient's health risk. Physicians, patients, and patient's relatives can benefit from the prediction's outcomes. In low resource clinical settings, it is necessary to predict the patient's condition after the admission to allocate resources appropriately. Several articles have been published analyzing the Prima Indian data set applying on various machine learning algorithms. Shankar applied neural networks to predict the onset of diabetes mellitus on the Prima Indian Diabetes dataset and showed that his approach for such classification is reliable. Machine learning techniques increase medical diagnosis accuracy and reduce medical cost.

There is no cure for diabetics but early detection can reduce the long term complications and reduce the cost. Millions of people in the world have diabetes. Many of these people do not even know whether they have it or not. The ability to predict diabetes early plays an important role for the patient's appropriate treatment strategy. However, the correct prediction accuracy of current machine learning algorithms is often low. LR performed the best among all 10 classifiers. It tried to predict whether an individual was diabetes positive or not.

Heart disease prediction with neural networks

Coronary heart disease is the number one cause of death in adults in the US, killing more than 370,000 Americans each year.

Technologies like the new Topological Analysis are used in combination with machine learning to analyze patient symptoms and deliver diagnoses with 95% accuracy. This is a great improvement from the current diagnosis done using stress echocardiograms that are only 80% accurate.

The heart attack is a common problem in all human beings above the age of 30. The cholesterol level is another major problem which leads to heart attacks. The knowledge discovery in databases is a well-defined process containing several distinct steps to get a perfect accuracy. Data mining is the core step, which results in the discovery of hidden information with useful knowledge. The discovered knowledge will be used by the healthcare administrators to predict some of the diseases and problems like heart attacks. Predicting patient's behavior in the future is the main application of data mining techniques. A formal definition of knowledge discovery in databases is given as follows: "Data mining is the non-trivial extraction of implicit previously unknown and potentially useful information about data."

Medical diagnosis is an important yet complicated task that needs to be done accurately and efficiently. The automation of this system is very much needed to help the physicians to do better diagnosis and treatment. Poor clinical decisions can lead to disastrous consequences which are therefore unacceptable. The major challenge of the healthcare system nowadays is to predict the diseases in a quality manner.

The clinical decisions made by doctors may be prone to errors and lead to some problems for patients. This system should be automated so that predicting the diseases is done accurately. One of the main problems in healthcare system is to predict the previous heart attacks of the patients. There are some techniques available to predict these things accurately. In most cases, the available data mining techniques are not used properly to predict the diseases in the healthcare systems. I can personally attest to that.

Other uses in healthcare

Algorithms are now being used for predictive analysis on the relationships between treatment and patient outcomes.

AI is widely used in healthcare, in areas such as diagnostic studies, drug development, patient monitoring, and palliative care.

Other important developments include the use of robots to effect precision surgery, character recognition technologies for converting medical records to electronic data, and big data analytics to provide personalized medicine.

There is a lot of regulation and bureaucracy about how the AI technologies can be allowed to carry out this instantaneous health-related and truly life-saving work.

Think about data access and licensing.

If government can create algorithms that can await API requests from hospitals, research bodies and institutions of higher learning, automatic approvals and licenses can greatly assist in the speedy deployment of current technologies and help to save lives.

Law and governance

Lawyering has many instances of repetitive work. Tasks like sifting through thousands of legal documents to find materials relevant for some piece of litigation have long been the cause of delayed cases which is mostly the cause of delayed justice.

Lawyers can also use AI systems to identify relevant entities in a legal undertaking like property development and issue legal documents, including notices and contracts.

Federal administrative tasks when done using traditional means have been ineffective, and slow at best, in making the right call.

Think of;

- Personal identification.

- Searching for lost individuals.

- Property ownership searches.

- Screening for criminals who use disguises to escape detection, especially at border points.

- Searching for personal information about suspects from international databases.

These are just but a few of federal tasks that can be done in an instant with the help of AI technologies.

How AI Is disrupting the law

It is difficult to read the news today without running across an article saying that AI will change everything. Is this also true of the legal profession? How will the practice of law and the provision of legal services change, if at all, in response to AI technology?

Some claim that we're in the midst of an "AI apocalypse:" that every level of society will be massively disrupted. Although much of this press is hype and click-bait, the reality within the practice of law is that AI is indeed beginning to have a substantial impact. Ultimately, AI will be more disruptive to the legal profession than the move in the last century from typewriters to word processors. For this reason, organizations that do not anticipate the changes being driven by AI today are likely to be left behind.

What is the source of this disruption? Simply put, AI software can analyze words: It can automatically classify and search for paragraphs, and compare documents and highlight changes. It can also learn over time from humans performing a task: AI/machine learning can use historical data to get started, then learn from human decisions going forward to continually improve its accuracy.

Multiple use cases

The most fertile area for AI in law to date is in handling boilerplate document completion and repetitive transactions. An example is the chatbot DoNotPay, called "the world's first robot lawyer." Originally intended to help users to fight parking tickets, it has today helped users contest more than 160,000 tickets across London and New York, all for free. DoNotPay's capabilities have now extended to new use cases: It helps people sue Equifax in small claims court and helps them identify when airplane ticket prices drop and obtain cash back. According to TechCrunch, the company is now "pushing out 1,000 new bots that can assist people in filling out transactional legal forms in all 50 U.S. states and the U.K."

Another example: JPMorgan's learning system, called COIN, short for COntract INtelligence. COIN analyzes a document in seconds, with fewer errors than humans, resulting in considerable cost savings. To date, it has replaced hundreds of thousands of human lawyer-hours in interpreting commercial loan agreements.

AI in context

Bill Fenwick is co-founder and currently Partner Emeritus of Fenwick and West LLP, which is based in Silicon Valley and has offices worldwide. Starting the firm that handled Apple's incorporation and Facebook's IPO, Fenwick has been a legal technology thought leader since the 1960s.

Speaking with Bill last month, he told us that AI will impact many aspects of the legal profession. These include defining what constitutes the practice of law: lawyers' rules of conduct, ethics, and malpractice, the duty to investigate, corporate law, taxation, and intellectual property, says Fenwick: "With AI, it will be quite possible to instantaneously predict the likely outcome of most disputes. What will it do to the function of judges and the judiciary? What will it do to government revenue systems? We know now, regardless of what's happening with the current administration, globalization is here to stay, and that involves hundreds of different countries' legal, social, economic and revenue systems."

A similar perspective comes from James A. Sherer, a partner in the New York office of BakerHostetler LLP, "…AI is already impacting current attorney practice in four discrete areas: (1) document review in e-discovery ("predictive coding" or technology-assisted review), (2) contract due diligence review in corporate transactions, (3) third-party legal research products in multiple practice areas, and (4) time entry and matter analysis."

Consider due diligence review. In the past, an attorney reviewing documentation for even a reasonably simple contract might need to consult previous similar contracts, searching for comparable language in the new document, as well as anomalous language or terminology. It's likely the attorney may have access to tools capable of conducting some word and phrase searching through these different contracts, at least partially highlighting distinctions and similarities, but it will be a human doing almost all of the analysis. This could take anywhere from a few hours to several weeks, depending on the complexity of the documents and the issues being faced.

With AI, however, a document can be reviewed in a matter of seconds, recognizing important language and issues and also finding and identifying those distinctions and similarities based on the previous contractual language from which the machine has been trained. In addition, the machine can distinguish between language involving the different areas requiring analysis, e.g., liability and indemnification, taxation, intellectual property, and insurance issues.

Note that AI is not doing legal work for the attorney but is "pre-filtering:" identifying factual and contextual analysis that gives the attorney information and clues as to where issues may arise in downstream negotiations or activities. AI software, having been trained on previously vetted documents and their nominal language, can compare the current document with all that it was previously trained on and determine where anomalies occur, thereby reducing the attorney's analysis time.

This "AI augmentation" arrangement—where the human and machine work hand-in-hand—is a proven pattern: It powered some of the earliest successful AI/machine vision systems in medicine. There, AI identified suspicious locations, possibly containing cancerous cells on pathology slides, which drastically reduced the workload for humans, who only had to examine suspicious slides and slide regions, instead of reviewing them all. According to one speaker at the time, this was like "going from reading an encyclopedia Britannica every day to just reading a few pages." Going forward, most legal use cases for AI will have a human in the loop in this way.

Keeping humans in the loop helps to mitigate the biggest challenge to AI in law. Says Fenwick: "the biggest problem with AI and the judicial system is the difficulty of creating the Trust (of citizens and institutions in its reliability) that will make the use of AI acceptable for dispute resolution."

In addition to changing how legal practice is conducted, AI is disrupting the shape of the legal ecosystem itself. The financial times books, "Change [from AI] is being driven not only by demand from clients but also by competition from accounting firms, which have begun to offer legal services and to use technology to do routine work. 'Lawtech' startups, often set up by ex-lawyers and so-called because they use technology to streamline or automate routine aspects of legal work, are a threat too."

Insurance

The insurance industry uses AI chatbots and virtual assistants for standard customer care Inquiries.

AI algorithms can also be deployed by insurance firms to detect fraudulent claims and carry out risk management.

Insurance firms can wade into predictive prevention applications through smart devices. For example, smart cameras can be used to caution against careless driving, give discounts to careful drivers or even activate contractual requirements.

But not all is rosy. Insurance firms, service providers, and the insured are notorious for fraudulent behaviour and outright crime in a bid to defraud the insurance process.

Sample this;

Intentional accidents in order to launch claims, which in themselves can, in turn, be exaggerated.

Claims from bogus medical practitioners can be bloated by mutual agreement between the practitioners and the insurance providers for compensation from the government.

Unnecessary treatment like increased cesarean deliveries can be sanctioned by hospitals.

Most of these fraudulent activities can deplete taxpayer funded insurance kitties and in the end negatively impact on the medical wellbeing of a country as a whole.

With AI's capability for detecting patterns, data pairs like comparisons between non-insured and insured health seekers' medical bills, analysing diagnostic books against practitioners' competence and simple patterns of serial insurance fraudsters to weed out any suspected claims can assist in minimizing this fraud.

Disaster management and data recovery

Using data mining, predictive analytics, and data optimization software, scientists are promising to be able to create high precision disaster management studies.

This will assist in the creation of mitigation plans to parry hitherto unavoidable public health crises like communicable diseases epidemics, hurricanes, and wildfires.

The data shared can be in many forms, including, but not limited to;

- Genetic mutation data mining to predict and pre-empt pathogen mutations and arm medics with accurate pre-emptive containment tactics.

- Use of GPS data using mobile phone telephony to track down, isolate, and quarantine suspected infected persons.

- Mapping highly precise substantial risk epidemic areas with human, animal, and environmental factors combined to create scenarios of where disease vectors might attack, spread to, and take hold, and therefore facilitate containment proactivity.

Data recovery

The government is primarily a service oriented entity, with hundreds of agencies and administrative units spread all over the country.

A lot of data is processed at these agencies, including personal and highly classified data sets that if lost, could prove very costly to the government, the agencies, corporates and individuals in general.

Some of the challenges that the government faces include natural disasters like floods, fires, and hurricanes that have the capability of wiping out entire neighbourhoods, and sensitive data can be lost this way.

There is also the existence of human-related calamities like terrorist attacks, data hacking, and war.

How can the government harness the power of AI to be better prepared for these unfortunate realities?

With the capability of data centres to use cloud connectivity, AI algorithms can be deployed to turn all data into an electronic format, and to automatically back it up in remote storage as a disaster mitigation plan.

CHAPTER 13
MAKING THE CASE FOR POLICY

As can be seen, there are many merits and demerits of unregulated AI. Companies are using AI to prevent and detect everything from routine employee theft to insider trading. Many banks and large corporations employ AI to detect and prevent fraud and money laundering. Social media companies use machine learning to block illicit content such as child pornography. Businesses are constantly experimenting with new ways to use AI for better risk management and faster, more responsive fraud detection — and even to predict and prevent crimes.

While today's basic technology is not necessarily revolutionary, the algorithms it uses and the results they can produce are. For instance, banks have been using transaction monitoring systems for decades based on pre-defined binary rules that require the output to be manually checked. The success rate is generally low: On average, only 2% of the transactions flagged by the systems ultimately reflect a true crime or malicious intent. By contrast, today's machine-learning solutions use predictive rules that automatically recognize anomalies in data sets. These advanced algorithms can significantly reduce the number of false alerts by filtering out cases that were flagged incorrectly, while uncovering others missed using conventional rules.

Given the wealth of data available today, and the rising expectations of customers and public authorities when it comes to protecting and managing that data, many companies have decided that this is one of the only ways to keep up with increasingly sophisticated criminals. Today, for example, social media companies are expected to uncover and remove terrorist recruitment videos and messages almost instantly. In time, AI-powered crime-fighting tools could become a requirement for large businesses, in part because there will be no other way to rapidly detect and interpret patterns across billions of pieces of data.

But determining whether AI crime-fighting solutions are a good strategic fit for a company depends on whether the benefits outweigh the risks that accompany them. One such risk is that biased conclusions can be drawn from AI based on factors like ethnicity, gender, and age. Companies can also experience backlash from customers who worry that their data will be misused or exploited by even more data-intensive surveillance of their records, transactions, and communications — especially if those insights are shared with the government. Recently, for example, a European bank was forced to backtrack on its plan to ask customers for permission to monitor their social media accounts as part of its mortgage application process, after a public outcry over its "Big Brother" tactics.

So how are leading-edge companies evaluating the benefits and risks of rapidly evolving AI crime-fighting and risk management?

Evaluating the strategic fit

Before embarking on an AI risk management initiative, managers must first understand where machine learning is already making a big difference. Banks, for example, are halting financial crimes much more quickly and cheaply than they used to by using AI for automating processes and conducting multilayered "deep learning" analyses. Even though banks now file 20 times more suspicious activity reports linked to money laundering than they did in 2012, AI tools have permitted them to shrink the armies of people they employ to evaluate alerts for suspicious activities. That's because their false alerts have fallen by as much as half thanks to AI, and because many banks are now able to automate routine human legwork in document evaluation. For example, using AI, PayPal has also cut its false alerts in half. And Royal Bank of Scotland prevented losses of over $9 million to customers after conducting a year-long pilot with Vocalink Analytics, a payments business, to use AI to scan small business transactions for fake invoices.

AI tools also allow companies to surface suspicious patterns or relationships invisible even to experts. For instance, artificial neural networks can enable employees to predict the next moves of even unidentified criminals who have figured out ways around alert triggers in binary rule-based security systems. These artificial neural networks link millions of data points from seemingly unrelated databases containing everything from social media posts to internet protocol addresses used on airport Wi-Fi networks to real estate holdings or tax returns, and identify patterns.

The next step in assessing the wisdom of launching an AI risk management program is for companies to evaluate to what extent customers and government authorities will expect them to be ahead of the curve. Even if it does not become a regulatory or legal obligation, companies might find it advantageous to play a leading role in the use of advanced analytics so they can take part in setting industrywide standards. They can help ensure that industry participants, regulators, technology innovators, and customers are being kept safe, without trampling on people's privacy and human rights.

Assessing and mitigating internal risks

As managers examine how AI can assist them in identifying criminal activities, they should also consider how it fits in with their broader AI strategy. AI risk management and crime detection should not be conducted in isolation. Back-testing against simpler models can help banks limit the impact of potentially inexplicable conclusions drawn by AI, especially if there is an unknown event for which the model has not been trained. For example, banks use AI to monitor transactions and reduce the number of false alerts they receive on potential rogue transactions, such as money that's being laundered for criminal purposes. These are back-tested against simpler rules-based models to identify potential outliers. An AI model may, for example, mistakenly overlook a large money laundering transaction that would normally trigger an alert in a rule-based system if it determines, based on biased data, that large transactions made by customers who reside in wealthy neighborhoods do not merit as much attention. Using this approach enables companies to design more transparent machine learning models, even if that means they operate within more explicit bounds.

Most of all, managers should assess whether their company's data analytics are sufficient to handle complex AI tools. If not, they need to develop data analytics capabilities in-house to reach a critical mass of automated processes and structured analytics.

Understanding and preparing for external risks

Increased use of AI tools for crime prevention could also cause external risks to cascade in unexpected ways. A company could lose its credibility with the public, regulators, and other stakeholders in a myriad ways — for example, if there are false alerts that mistakenly identify people as "suspicious" or "criminal" due to a racial bias unintentionally built into the system. Or at the other end of the spectrum, if they miss criminal activities, like drug trafficking conducted by their clients or funds channeled from sanctioned countries such as Iran. Criminals could resort to more extreme, and potentially violent, measures to outmaneuver AI. Customers could flee to less closely monitored entities outside of regulated industries. A moral hazard could even develop if employees become too reliant on AI crime-fighting tools to catch criminals for them.

To prevent this from happening, companies need to create and test a variety of scenarios of cascading events resulting from AI-driven tools used to track criminal activities. To outsmart money launderers, for example, banks should conduct "war games" with ex-prosecutors and investigators to discover how they would beat their system.

With results produced through scenario analysis, managers can then help top executives and board members decide how comfortable they are with using AI crime-fighting. They can also develop crisis management playbooks containing internal and external communication strategies so they can react swiftly when things (inevitably) go wrong.

By using AI, companies can identify areas of potential crimes such as fraud, money laundering, and terrorist financing — in addition to more mundane crimes such as employee theft, cyber fraud, and fake invoices — to help public agencies with prosecuting these offenses much more effectively and efficiently. But with these benefits come risks that should be openly, honestly, and transparently assessed to determine whether using AI in this way is a strategic fit. It will not be easy. But clear communication with regulators and customers will allow companies to rise to the challenge when things go wrong. AI will eventually have a hugely positive impact on reducing crime in the world — as long as it is managed well.

Developing Direct/Indirect Policy on AI

The jury is still out about whether to develop direct policy on AI or not, and how urgently this is needed.

There are two schools of thought;

The dissenters

To some, the idea of creating policy to govern the deployment of AI technologies seem premature. They argue that regulation could stifle the very development of the technologies.

Interestingly, most of these entities have hugely benefitted from both legal and unethical use of these technologies to amass unbelievable fortunes in very short timelines.

From creating marketing algorithms that use AI to profile potential buyers to stream advertisements to creating smart devices, they have created the biggest companies by market capitalization in the world.

Demis Hassabis, CEO of Google DeepMind, and Andrew McAfee are on record in stating that it is way too early for an explicit AI Policy.

They claim that the technology is still nascent and that research should first be supported and encouraged.

The proponents

But this notion is flawed. If global giants like Google, Facebook and Apple depend on this technology for their core businesses, then AI is not nascent any more.

The horse has bolted. This technology is impacting the lives of billions of people many trillions of times each day.

And the ugly side of the technology is now clear for all to see. In fact, technology does not need to flourish before the policy is developed.

It is actually better to regulate from the get-go so that boundaries can be set, and the entrenchment of its dangerous manifestations can be contained as early as possible.

This is why governments are now starting to make efforts to ensure that this technology is channelled for the benefit of all.

Addressing societal impact

Most of the technologies involved in AI are still under experimentation, and firmly under the control of a select number of global conglomerates like Alphabet and Microsoft.

Due to the monopolized nature of these advances, it is hard for governments to keep an oversight of technologies that are only just being understood, and which are currently kept in black boxes labelled as 'trade secrets.'

Already, there has been public fallouts due to privacy trust issues caused by the use of AI on massive personal information databases collected by these IT behemoths and converted into colossal revenue streams like personalized marketing.

There is also the legal (and sometimes not so legal) efforts to lock out competition in areas like retail due to unfair deployment of these technologies to deny smaller players access to otherwise open source facilities that enable them to carry out normal business.

Just what can these companies do with your data?

And how can regulation address these concerns while leveling the playing field with democratization of these technologies?

Potential risks from advanced AI systems

Loss of control of very powerful AI systems: AI systems will likely become much more capable across a broad range of environments, making them much more effective at achieving their specified goals in creative ways. However, designing AI systems that can be meaningfully controlled by humans and that reliably avoid negative side-effects may be challenging, especially if AI systems' capabilities and the range of possible side-effects outpaces humans' ability to foresee them. Incautiously designed systems might reasonably model human attempts to constrain them as obstacles to be overcome, and very capable AI systems pursuing problematic goals may become exceedingly difficult for humans to control; AI systems with this issue could be reasonably expected to create difficulties at least comparable to those created by today's computer worms or cybercrime organizations (and plausibly much greater difficulties). If AI systems with problematic goals become sufficiently capable, their pursuit of those goals could significantly harm humanity's long-term future, and it seems to us that there is a non-negligible chance of outcomes as bad as human extinction.

Gradual loss of meaningful control of society's direction: As more and more control is gradually ceded to complex and hard-to-understand AI systems that pursue imperfect proxies of different goals (e.g. maximizing profit), humans may lose the ability to make meaningful collective choices about what direction society should take. Emerging concerns about AI systems that discriminate based on e.g. race or gender could be an early example of such a dynamic, as could concerns about filter bubbles created by increased tailoring of news stories to individuals' predicted tastes. If the technical ability to design systems that faithfully and transparently reflect human values lags far behind the ability to profitably automate decision-making, this could pose long-term problems for the trajectory of civilization.

Moral relevance of AI systems: At present, there exists very little consensus on what kind of non-human beings count as "morally relevant" (chimpanzees? Pigs? Ants?). I find it plausible, though by no means definite, that some AI systems may at some point become morally relevant in some meaningful sense. If this were to come about, it could have very significant implications for how AI systems should be designed and used, potentially requiring some protections for certain AI agents. For example, it might be possible to duplicate AI "workers" cheaply; if so, this would drive down the cost of labor that these workers could perform (since new workers could always be generated), potentially creating a situation in which AI "workers" are only able to earn subsistence wages (e.g., enough to cover hardware and power costs). The extent to which situations like this are worth avoiding is tightly connected to the extent to which AI systems have moral worth and/or are entitled to some equivalent of human rights.

CHAPTER 14
OVERRIDING POLICY FORMULATION PRINCIPLE

To realize a well-coordinated AI universe, several things must be done right, and in a coordinated manner.

For starters, the world must agree to have some guiding principles that allow for a constructive approach to the development of these technologies. These principles can go along the following lines...

- That science and policy always work hand in hand to develop sound policies in line with accepted technologies.

- That AI teams work in cooperation to avoid a technological race and wastage due to duplication of efforts

- That effort is only channelled for the common good of all humanity.

- That the liability of the safety risks of AI technologies be owned by the companies that has developed the technology.

AI ideal governance - key considerations

As machine learning algorithms are used in more and more products and services, there are some serious factors that must be considered when addressing AI, particularly in the context of people's trust in the Internet:

Socio-Economic Impacts

The new functions and services of AI are expected to have significant socio-economic impacts. The ability of machines to exhibit advanced cognitive skills to process natural language, to learn, to plan and to perceive, makes it possible for new tasks to be performed by intelligent systems, sometimes with more success than humans. New applications of AI could open up exciting opportunities for more effective medical care, safer industries and services, and boost productivity on a massive scale.

Transparency, bias, and accountability

AI-made decisions can have serious impacts in people's lives. AI may discriminate against some individuals or make errors due to biased training data. How a decision is made by AI is often hard to understand, making problems of bias harder to solve and ensuring accountability much more difficult.

New uses for data

Machine learning algorithms have proved efficient in analyzing and identifying patterns in large amounts of data, commonly referred to as "Big Data." Big Data is used to train learning algorithms to increase their performance. This generates an increasing demand for data, encouraging data collection and raising risks of oversharing of information at the expense of user privacy.

Security and safety

Advances in AI and its use will also create new security and safety challenges. These include unpredictable and harmful behavior of the AI agent, but also adversarial learning by malicious actors.

Ethics

AI may make choices that could be deemed unethical, yet also be a logical outcome of the algorithm, emphasizing the importance of building in ethical considerations into AI systems and algorithms.

New ecosystems

Like the impact of mobile Internet, AI makes new applications, services, and new means of interacting with the network possible. For example, through speech and smart agents, this may create new challenges to how open or accessible the Internet becomes.

Types of AI environments

When designing AI solutions, we spend a lot of time focusing on aspects such as the nature of learning algorithms [ex: supervised, unsupervised, semi-supervised] or the characteristics of the data [ex: classified, unclassified...]. However, little attention is often provided to the nature of the environment on which the AI solution operates. As it turns out, the characteristics of the environment are one of the absolutely key elements to determine the right models for an AI solution.

There are several aspects that distinguish AI environments. The shape and frequency of the data, the nature of the problem, and the volume of knowledge available at any given time are some of the elements that differentiate one type of AI environment from another. Understanding the characteristics of the AI environment is one of the first tasks that AI practitioners focused on to tackle a specific AI problem. From that perspective, there are several categories I use to group AI problems based on the nature of the environment.

Complete vs. incomplete

Complete AI environments are those which, at any given time, have enough information to complete a branch of the problem. Chess is a classic example of a complete AI environment. Poker, on the other hand, is an incomplete environment as AI strategies cannot anticipate many moves in advance and, instead, they focus on finding a good 'equilibrium" at any given time.

Fully observable vs. partially observable

A fully observable AI environment has access to all required information to complete its target task. Image recognition operates in fully observable domains. Partially observable environments such as the ones encountered in self-driving vehicle scenarios deal with partial information to solve AI problems.

Competitive vs. collaborative

Competitive AI environments face AI agents against each other to optimize a specific outcome. Games such as GO or Chess are examples of competitive AI environments. Collaborative AI environments rely on the cooperation between multiple AI agents. Self-driving vehicles cooperating to avoid collisions or smart home sensor interactions are examples of collaborative AI environments.

Static vs. dynamic

Static AI environments rely on data-knowledge sources that don't change frequently over time. Speech analysis is a problem that operates on static AI environments. Contrasting with that model, dynamic AI environments such as the vision AI systems in drones that deal with data sources that change quite frequently.

Discrete vs. continuous

Discrete AI environments are those on which a finite [although arbitrarily large] set of possibilities can drive the outcome of the task. Chess is also classified as a discrete AI problem. Continuous AI environments rely on unknown and rapidly changing data sources. Vision systems in drones or self-driving cars operate in continuous AI environments.

Deterministic vs. stochastic

Deterministic AI environments are those on which the outcome can be determined based on a specific state. In other words, deterministic environments ignore uncertainty. Most real world AI environments are not deterministic. Instead, they can be classified as stochastic. Self-driving vehicles are a classic example of stochastic AI processes.

CHAPTER 15
POLICY FORMULATION FOR AI CONTROL

With this in mind, it is possible to think of the best ways of developing policy.

Addressing information asymmetries

Even though experts in the AI field are heavily compensated in the private sector, regulatory authorities can find other ways of incorporating industry experts in government, starting with temporary 'tours of duty' and consultation when formulating policy.

Reduce regulatory friction with industry experts by encouraging flexibility in regulatory bureaucracy and self-regulation.

Obtain hand-on experiences by visiting labs and companies, attending symposiums and seminars that disambiguate the technologies and work in collaboration with other jurisdictions that are ahead in policy design.

Foster public-private partnerships

Expert stakeholders must be drawn from academia, industry, and among the rank and file in government controlled institutions to address the challenges that must come into play when policy is being developed.

Governments must create a robust interrelationship in the fraternity to foster mutual trust and openness.

Fund AI-based research

To take a front seat at the high table of AI knowledge, governments must also show a keen interest in sponsoring efforts towards AI research.

Elementary curricula must be developed and incorporated into Schools.

Degree courses that have detailed AI based technologies in their catalogues must be encouraged in universities. Governments must start showing an interest in how these courses are structured and what content is used for instruction.

Create an international AI governance authority

Jurisdictional discretion must be sacrificed at the altar of intergovernmental cooperation to avoid duplication and AI racing which in itself is the single most dangerous after-effect of lack of cooperation in new technological advances.

Governments must work towards full regulatory disclosure from all parties experimenting with AI on the global scale to assure the majority that regulators are watching out for the ethical deployment of the technologies.

This can be achieved by the creation of a global AI governance body.

And it must be given both prosecutorial and investigative powers to pry and scrutinize on-going development.

Its composition must be multi-sectorial and bipartisan, allowing regulators and industry to come together to coordinate international policy.

Create an international code of practice for benchmarking

Efforts in the US, together with other efforts from Europe, Canada, the UK, China and the rest of the world must be used to create an international Code of Practice under the auspices of an existent international governing body to govern AI development.

This body is the IAAIL (the international Association for AI and Law).

A lot of this work is already under way through the IAAIL's coordinated conferences known as ICAIL. The next one is in April 2019 in Montreal, Canada.

This code of practice must be reviewed at a frequency that is determined by the exigencies identified by the stakeholders in the AI community in a bid to avoid lame duck regulations in the face of rapid AI advancement, while still allowing for the standards to be understood and implemented before they are reviewed again.

Major policy formation take away

AI has the potential to disrupt virtually all sectors in a big and positive way.

However, left unchecked, there are many risks posed by the creation of intelligent machines.

And policy making is not easy especially when it comes to a group of technologies that are still being defined in terms of form and depth.

However, with proper coordination and forward-looking, inclusive and exhaustive Intra and intergovernmental efforts, proper and adequate policy can be developed to assure the development of safe and ethical technologies that do not pose a threat to mankind.

CHAPTER 16

GUIDING PRINCIPLES AND RECOMMENDATIONS

While the deployment of AI in Internet based services is not new, the current trend point to AI as an increasingly important factor in the Internet's future development and use. As such, these guiding principles and recommendations are a first attempt to guide the debate going forward. Furthermore, while this paper is focused on the specific challenges surrounding AI, the strong interdependence between its development and the expansion of the Internet of Things (IoT) demands a closer look at interoperability and security of IoT devices.

Ethical considerations in deployment and design

Principle: AI system designers and builders need to apply a user-centric approach to the technology. They need to consider their collective responsibility in building AI systems that will not pose security risks to the Internet and Internet users.

Recommendations:

- Adopt ethical standards: Adherence to the principles and standards of ethical considerations in the design of AI, should guide researchers and industry going forward.

- Promote ethical considerations in innovation policies: Innovation policies should require adherence to ethical standards as a pre-requisite for things like funding.

Ensure "interpretability" of AI systems

Principle: Decisions made by an AI agent should be possible to understand, especially if those decisions have implications for public safety, or result in discriminatory practices.

Recommendations:

- Ensure Human Interpretability of Algorithmic Decisions: AI systems must be designed with the minimum requirement that the designer can account for an AI agent's behaviors. Some systems with potentially severe implications for public safety should also have the functionality to provide information in the event of an accident.

- Empower Users: Providers of services that utilize AI need to incorporate the ability for the user to request and receive basic explanations as to why a decision was made.

Public Empowerment

Principle: The public's ability to understand AI-enabled services, and how they work, is key to ensuring trust in the technology.

Recommendations:

- "Algorithmic Literacy" must be a basic skill: Whether it is the curating of information in social media platforms or self-driving cars, users need to be aware and have a basic understanding of the role of algorithms and autonomous decision-making. Such skills will also be important in shaping societal norms around the use of the technology, for example, identifying decisions that may not be suitable to delegate to an AI.

- Provide the public with information: While full transparency around a service's machine learning techniques and training data is generally not advisable due to the security risk, the public should be provided with enough information to make it possible for people to question its outcomes.

Responsible Deployment

Principle: The capacity of an AI agent to act autonomously, and to adapt its behavior over time without human direction, calls for significant safety checks before deployment, and ongoing monitoring.

Recommendations:

- Humans must be in control: Any autonomous system must allow for a human to interrupt an activity or shutdown the system (an "off-switch"). There may also be a need to incorporate human checks on new decision-making strategies in AI system design, especially where the risk to human life and safety is great.

- Make safety a priority: Any deployment of an autonomous system should be extensively tested beforehand to ensure the AI agent's safe interaction with its environment (digital or physical) and that it functions as intended. Autonomous systems should be monitored while in operation, and updated or corrected as needed.

- Privacy is key: AI systems must be data responsible. They should use only what they need and delete it when it is no longer needed ("data minimization"). They should encrypt data in transit and at rest, and restrict access to authorized persons ("access control"). AI systems should only collect, use, share, and store data in accordance with privacy and personal data laws and best practices.

- Think before you act: Careful thought should be given to the instructions and data provided to AI systems. AI systems should not be trained with data that is biased, inaccurate, incomplete or misleading.

- If they are connected, they must be secured: AI systems that are connected to the Internet should be secured not only for their protection, but also to protect the Internet from malfunctioning or malware-infected AI systems that could become the next-generation of botnets. High standards of device, system and network security should be applied.

- Responsible disclosure: Security researchers acting in good faith should be able to responsibly test the security of AI systems without fear of prosecution or other legal action. At the same time, researchers and others who discover security vulnerabilities or other design flaws should responsibly disclose their findings to those who are in the best position to fix the problem.

Ensuring accountability

<u>Principle:</u> Legal accountability has to be ensured when human agency is replaced by decisions of AI agents.

<u>Recommendations:</u>

- Ensure legal certainty: Governments should ensure legal certainty on how existing laws and policies apply to algorithmic decision-making and the use of autonomous systems to ensure a predictable legal environment. This includes working with experts from all disciplines to identify potential gaps and run legal scenarios. Similarly, those designing and using AI should be in compliance with existing legal frameworks.

- Put users first: Policymakers need to ensure that any laws applicable to AI systems and their use put users' interests at the center. This must include the ability for users to challenge autonomous decisions that adversely affect their interests.

- Assign liability up-front: Governments working with all stakeholders need to make some difficult decisions now about who will be liable in the event that something goes wrong with an AI system, and how any harm suffered will be remedied.

Social And Economic Impacts

Principle: Stakeholders should shape an environment where AI provides socio-economic opportunities for all.

Recommendations:

- All stakeholders should engage in an ongoing dialogue to determine the strategies needed to seize upon AI's vast socio-economic opportunities for all, while mitigating its potential negative impacts. A dialogue could address related issues such as educational reform, universal income, and a review of social services.

Open governance

Principle: The ability of various stakeholders, whether civil society, government, private sector or academia and the technical community, to inform and participate in the governance of AI is crucial for its safe deployment.

Recommendations:

- Promote Multi-stakeholder Governance: Organizations, institutions and processes related to the governance of AI need to adopt an open, transparent and inclusive approach. It should be based on four key attributes: Inclusiveness and transparency; Collective responsibility; Effective decision making and implementation and Collaboration through distributed and interoperable governance.

CHAPTER 17
THE KEY ASPECTS OF AI POLICY

AI policy changes from country to country. Depending on a country's national strengths and weaknesses, a government will choose to focus on different aspects of AI policy. Finland, for instance, wants to lead the world in the application of AI technologies, while Canada wants to be the global leader in AI research and training. The United States has taken a free-market approach to AI policy, while China has implemented a comprehensive, nationwide approach.

Despite these differences, AI policy can essentially be broken down into the following ten categories:

1. Basic and applied research

To achieve new breakthroughs in AI theories, technologies, and applications, governments need to provide funding for basic and applied research. This includes both research grants and the creation of new research institutions. Example: the UK's Alan Turing Institute.

2. Talent attraction, development, and retention

To conduct R&D in AI and deploy AI solutions in the public and private sectors, countries need a supply of skilled AI talent. Example: Canada's CIFAR Chairs in AI Program.

3. Future of work and skills

Advances in AI will both create and destroy jobs. To ensure that workers have the skills to compete in the digital economy, governments need to invest in STEM education, national retraining programs, and lifelong learning. Example: Denmark's Technology Pact.

4. Industrialization of AI technologies

AI has the potential to fundamentally transform multiple sectors and drive growth for decades to come. To encourage private sector uptake, governments are investing in strategic sectors and developing AI ecosystems and clusters. Example: Japan's Industrialization Roadmap.

5. AI in the government

Likewise, governments are experimenting with ways to encourage the uptake of AI in the government. With the help of AI, it is possible to reform the public administration and make policy more effective. Example: UAE's Ministry of AI.

6. Data and digital infrastructure

Data is central to the ability of AI to work. As a result, governments are opening their datasets and developing platforms to encourage the secure exchange of private data. Example: France's Health Data Hub.

7. Ethics

Concerns over algorithmic bias, privacy, and security have raised a number of ethical debates. To mitigate harm, governments are looking to develop ethical codes and standards for the use and development of AI. Example: The EU's Draft AI Ethics Guidelines.

8. Regulations

Every country is grappling with the question of whether (and how) to regulate AI. Currently, governments are focused on regulations for autonomous cars and autonomous weapons. Example: Germany's Ethics Commission on Automated and Connected Driving.

9. Inclusion

AI can both improve and worsen inclusion. Used properly, AI can bolster inclusion and help address complex societal problems such as poverty and hunger. Used improperly, AI can reinforce discrimination and disproportionately harm women and minorities. Example: India's #AIforAll Strategy.

10. Foreign Policy

Geopolitics, development, and trade will all be affected by advances in AI technologies. To address ethical concerns and develop global standards, countries are beginning to consider mechanisms for the global governance of AI. Example: China's Global Governance of AI Plan.

Key Takeaways

- AI policy is about maximizing AI's many benefits for your economy and societies while minimizing its risks and harms.

- Technological advancement in AI can only partially explain the sudden interest in AI policy. Governments are also keenly aware of the limited supply of AI talent and investment and are trying to get ahead of the new challenges caused by AI.

- Governments in all regions of the world are experimenting with AI policy. Currently, there is no best practice since the field is so new. However, AI policy can be broken down into ten categories: basic and applied research; talent attraction, development, and retention; future of work and skills; industrialization of AI technologies; AI in the government; data and digital infrastructure; ethics; regulations; inclusion; and foreign policy.

CONCLUSION

There are already many practical efforts underway that will advance your understanding and use of AI. Within government, GDS (Government Digital Service) is leading the way in developing digital skills, establishing what responsible practice looks like through the Data Science Ethical Framework, and developing your institutional skill in using AI for the benefit of the UK. And I will continue to invest in key research areas, and work with businesses to encourage inward investment, helping people to establish a global lead in the development and implementation of AI.

Reaping the benefits of this revolution in information technology will require an approach to ethics and governance that enables innovation, builds trust among citizens, establishes a stable environment for businesses and investors, and fosters appropriate access to the data necessary for computer science to develop this technology still further. It is important that government actively works to bring this about.

The right form of governance for AI, and indeed for the use of digital data more widely, is not self-evident. It is important to consider forms of data governance that cover all elements of the increasingly complex space, from responsibly generating data from people's behavior to remaining accountable for autonomous software agents. Additionally, any approach adopted must be flexible, able to adapt to new uses and more advanced forms of AI. There are many models that can be considered. But the important task is to set out what needs to be done before considering how it is to be achieved.

Learning from experience

While machines are increasingly capable of learning from experience, governments at times seem to begin governing modern technologies anew without learning from other relevant cases. And despite the clear signs that AI is developing quickly, diffusing rapidly, and likely to continue having substantial societal impacts well into the future, there has yet been no substantial effort to improve U.S. government capacity to appropriately govern AI. As of the time of writing, the White House's exploration into the issue remains in an information-gathering stage—we hope they and other policymakers will consider some of the recommendations below when deciding on bolder next steps. My recommendations are organized around several core areas in which de facto AI policy is currently lacking.

First, there is the question of government expertise in AI. The most important and obvious thing that governments should do to increase their capacity to sensibly govern AI is to improve their expertise on the matter through policy changes that will support more talent and the formation of an agency to coordinate AI policy. It is widely recognized that governments are currently ill-equipped to deal with ongoing AI developments. A telling example of this deficit is that NASA had to be brought into aid the Department of Transportation in investigating reports of unintended acceleration due to Toyota cars' control systems. This incapacity has two forms: dispersion of expertise across many agencies, and the low level of overall expertise even when adding up all those people. To some extent, dispersion is inevitable and desirable —many agencies deals with AI-relevant policy issues, and it would be undesirable to concentrate all of the experts in one place as a result.

However, compelling arguments have been made by legal scholar Ryan Calo that a Federal Robotics Commission would be appropriate for coordinating governance of robotics and accelerating the accumulation of federal expertise in robotics. Majority support something along such lines for AI more generally, given the close connections between AI and robotics, perhaps a Federal AI and Robotics Commission would be an appropriate title for an agency addressing both areas and their many intersections. The long history of governance of emerging technologies suggests that new agencies can play a constructive role in partially centralizing expertise in a topic, improving coordination, and clarifying the allocation of responsibilities. Many important questions have been raised about how such an agency should be designed, where in the government it should sit, and what its responsibilities should be.

The other aspect of government's lack of expertise, the total amount of expertise in government as opposed to its dispersion or concentration, is perhaps more challenging to address. But here, too, there are useful precedents. The challenge is partly one of incentives –AI is a very hot commercial and academic area right now, and salaries available in industry greatly exceed those in government. Moreover, while some agencies have recently made great strides on the closely-related issue of the prestige of government jobs; for example, through dynamic and mission-oriented agencies like the U.S. Digital Service. Most of the top students in AI still presently go to academic and industry jobs rather than choosing to serve in government. This can be addressed in part by learning from the experience of other agencies, such as the Advanced Research Projects Agency –Energy (ARPA-E), the legislation for which specifically enables it to hire top talent rapidly and at competitive salaries.

Thus, while there are steps that can be taken by the "Executive Branch" today to improve capacity in AI, tailored legislation may be needed to scale up government AI expertise by bypassing byzantine hiring policies that deter people from considering government jobs when easier-to-obtain and higher-paying jobs are available elsewhere. And while pursuing direct employment of AI experts by the government is important, developing innovative ways of tapping into the outside expertise of industry and academia can be pursued in parallel, in recognition of the partially-inherent difficulties outlined above.

The second key area for improvement in AI policy is in the funding of research. While there is much to praise about current AI funding policies in the U.S., such as their critical role in supporting basic research and graduate student training, there are several ways in which funding policies could be improved. First, the U.S. should substantially increase the share of civilian AI research relative to defense and intelligence AI research. The latter, while often useful for the reasons outlined earlier, is less likely to address significant societal problems in the areas like health and energy than funding specifically targeted at such problems. Of course, there is significant private funding available for AI research, but most of these are provided either directly or indirectly in a commercial setting. Particularly for research concerning the possible impacts of commercial AI on society, more neutral funding directly accountable to voters may be of use.

Many AI researchers in the United States pursue pro-social research on their own time or on the few grants available for such purposes, but many others (sometimes grudgingly) rely on military and intelligence funding. Besides providing additional options to researchers, additional civilian funding would provide an opportunity for concerted efforts–coordinated across agencies–to tackle societal problems in part through the development and diffusion of AI.

Second, research agencies should dedicate funding to research the ethical, policy, and safety issues raised by AI. To date, much of such research is done by researchers on their own time, or through private investments. Again, this is a clear area where government should support the production of public goods, such as insights into risks and opportunities of AI, means of safely controlling advanced AI systems, research on transparency and understanding of AI systems, and technological forecasting. Additionally, work on the ethics of AI and the policy issues surrounding it, ranging from privacy to potential security risks, should be more actively supported. While such research would be broadly beneficial, it is not currently being pursued by more than a handful of unusually forward-thinking companies and think tanks, and a few government-funded projects.

Importantly, in funding such research, agencies should learn from the experiences of the Human Genome Project, in which Ethical, Legal, and Social Implications (ELSI) research was widely regarded as not having affected either policy or ongoing technical research. In contrast, AI research in ethics, policy, forecasting, safety, and other areas should, to the extent possible, be integrated into technical research projects, supporting truly needed interdisciplinary research. Research grants should include provisions for, and additional earmarked funding to support, ethical training for undergraduate and graduate student researchers. While some AI researchers are proactive about raising ethical issues in their classrooms and laboratories, and there is effort in AI at the federal level to ensure such training, many students enter industry and research positions with little awareness of the complex ethical dilemmas they may face. Such investments and mandates should include pilot programs to pursue innovative approaches to integrating ethics into AI curricula, and should learn from the experiences of prior efforts in other areas such as biology.

A third area for policy research improvement relates to the diffusion of AI technologies. As you can learn from domains like health care and energy technologies, it is not sufficient to fund basic research and expect it to be widely and equitably diffused in society by private actors. In energy, a long history of experience tells us that public-private demonstration projects, tax incentives, and other approaches are critical complements to basic research funding. In the case of AI, what's notable is the generality of AI techniques. With sufficient expertise, they can be applied to virtually any domain, but if private industry leads diffusion of such technologies, you can expect a deficit in areas where AI may not quickly save large amounts of money, or lead to a sustainable business. Yet such areas may be of critical social value—for example, in areas of poverty alleviation, rare diseases, and accelerating clean energy technologies. AI in this sense is somewhat analogous to electricity, as argued by AI luminary Andrew Ng –it can increase productivity in a wide range of areas, but what often goes unmentioned in this analogy is that it took many decades for electricity to reach some markets, and indeed, over a billion still lack access to it.

Currently, we see large amounts of money flowing into AI research and development, but much of that investment is concentrated in a few key domains like driverless cars. The scarcity of expertise makes it conceivable that the majority of the societal potential of AI will go untapped for well into the future. Fortunately, there are encouraging case studies that suggest a different approach to diffusing AI, and they may provide government with leverage to simultaneously make progress on the ethical and safety fronts discussed earlier. Specifically, the U.S. federal government could develop a new agency inspired by agricultural extension services and the Manufacturing Extension Partnership (MEP). A so-called AI Extension Service, or something similar, could fulfill three functions simultaneously.

First, it could provide a point of contact for non-profits, local governments, and small businesses that lack AI expertise to seek out assistance with developing AI applications appropriate to their needs, providing a complement to industry that can focus more on unprofitable or especially societally important areas that are unlikely to be addressed by private forces alone, or require more public trust or long-term stability than any individual corporation can provide. Second, such an agency could aid with the expertise gap outlined earlier, by providing an exciting career path for AI experts, in which in the industry they can help people solve real problems, but for a wider range of problems than they might be exposed to when profitability necessarily guides decision-making.

Already, the U.S. Digital Service has effectively recruited many top IT experts to public service with a similarly exciting mission, though focused on improving government processes rather than serving non-government entities, and without a strong AI focus. An AI Extension Service could either be an additional growth area for that agency or an inspiration for a more AI focused, outward-looking agency. Third, by serving as a repository of expertise, such an agency would have the ability to influence the specific means by which AI is adopted in the marketplace –for example, the ethical and safety standards, the transparency of AI systems, and user and public engagement in developing the systems. Depending on on the scale of this initiative, such an effort may or may not affect a large share of AI applications directly, but it could at the very least serve as an exemplar for private projects, and a proving ground for best practices.

The fourth and final area of AI policy we'll discuss involves planning for the future. While much is known about the state of the art in AI today and how it might evolve in the near future, there are still substantial uncertainties. No one knows for certain, for example, when and whether AI systems will be able to broadly compete with human intelligence across a wide range of cognitive areas –and yet, this uncertainty does not mean you should ignore such a possibility. Rather, I suggest that a Federal AI and Robotics Commission, or existing institutions like the White House Office of Science and Technology Policy, coordinate an on-going government-wide initiative to investigate possible AI futures, drawing on the best methods in technological forecasting and scenario planning, and to also investigate both how agencies can leverage such technologies for the public good, and how critical mission areas could be affected by AI and then adjust policy based on such futures.

Example: in the case of the Department of Education, preparing future workers and citizens for coexistence with and enhancement by AI. The goal here should not be picking one preferred future and seeking to achieve or adapt to it; though, of course, agencies should be proactive but rather seeking robustness and preparedness in the face of uncertainty.

Toward smart AI policies

In this research, the nature of AI and why AI is of critical social importance has been reviewed. I have refuted the claim that it is too early for government policy intervention in AI by showing its extensive existing impact on society, and the broad range of policy already affecting AI's development and dissemination. And Furthermore, I have made specific policy recommendations based on lessons learned both positive and negative from previous government support and intervention in important technologies, such as energy and the human genome. Many issues have not been addressed here, such as how and to what extent to democratize AI policy—how can we ensure that citizens can play a role in influencing the development of these systems which already influence them so heavily? And how can we ensure that humans remain accountable for the actions of AI systems, while also fostering continued innovation in areas where autonomously acting systems can have significant societal benefits, such as autonomous cars? These are just some of the questions that remain. But by taking the steps I suggest—building expertise in government, more thoughtfully funding research, creating specific agencies to monitor and encourage social impact, taking a proactive approach to diffusing AI technologies, and generally planning better for the future—the government can provide a foundation for a robust, forward-looking AI policy system. Building on these recommendations, I believe national and transnational governments can help society to reap the benefits while reducing the downsides of AI.

SOURCES AND REFERENCES

1. Agrawal, A, J Gans, and A Goldfarb (2018b), Prediction Machines: The Simple Economics of AI, Harvard Business School Press.
2. Agrawal, A, J Gans, and A Goldfarb (2018a), "Economic Policy for AI", NBER Working Paper 24690.
3. Agrawal, A, J Gans, and A Goldfarb (eds) (2018c), The Economics of AI: An Agenda, University of Chicago Press.
4. Agrawal, A, J McHale, and A Oettl (2018), "Finding Needles in Haystacks: AI and Recombinant Growth", in A Agrawal, J Gans, and A Goldfarb (eds), The Economics of AI: An Agenda, University of Chicago Press.
5. Amitai Etzioni and Oren Etzioni, "Keeping AI Legal," Vanderbilt Journal of Entertainment & Technology Law 19, no. 1 (2016).
6. Arkin, Ronald. Governing lethal behavior in autonomous robots. Chapman and Hall/CRC, 2009.
7. Acemoglu, D, and P Restrepo (2018), "AI, Automation and Work", in A Agrawal, J Gans, and A Goldfarb (eds), The Economics of AI: An Agenda, University of Chicago Press.
8. Bengio, Y., Ducharme, R., Vincent, P. & Janvin, C. A neural probabilistic language model. J. Mach. Learn. Res. 3, 1137–1155 (2003).
9. Bishop, C. M. Pattern Recognition and Machine Learning (Springer, 2006).
Murphy, K. P. Machine Learning: A Probabilistic Perspective (MIT Press, 2012).

10. Bryson, J. 2016. "Patiencyis Not a Virtue: AI and the Design of Ethical Systems," Proceedings of AAAI 2016.
11. Brynjolfsson, E. and McAfee, A. 2014. The Second Machine Age: Work, Progress, and Prosperity in a Time of Brilliant Technologies. New York: W.W. Norton & Company.
12. Cox, R. T. The Algebra of Probable Inference (Johns Hopkins Univ. Press, 1961).
13. Calo, R. 2014. "The Case for a Federal Robotics Commission," Brookings Institution.
14. Calo, R., Froomkin, A. M., and Kerr, I. eds. 2016. Robot Law. Cheltenham: Edward Elgar Publishing.
15. Cockburn, I, R Henderson, and S Stern (2018), "The Impact of AI on Innovation", in A Agrawal, J Gans, and A Goldfarb (eds), The Economics of AI: An Agenda, University of Chicago Press.
16. De Finetti, B. La prévision: ses lois logiques, ses sources subjectives. In Annales de l'institut Henri Poincaré
17. Deneve, S. Bayesian spiking neurons I: inference. Neural Comput. 20, 91–117 (2008).
18. Doucet, A., de Freitas, J. F. G. & Gordon, N. J. Sequential Monte Carlo Methods in Practice (Springer, 2000). Minka, T. P. Expectation propagation for approximate Bayesian inference. In Proc. Uncertainty in Artificial Intelligence 17 362–369 (2001).
19. Doya, K., Ishii, S., Pouget, A. & Rao, R. P. N. Bayesian Brain: Probabilistic Approaches to Neural Coding (MIT Press, 2007).
20. Dutton, Tim (2018). "An Overview of National AI Strategies." Politics + AI, Medium.

21. Erik Brynjolfsson and Andrew McAfee, The Second Machine Age: Work, Progress, and Prosperity in a Time of Brilliant Technologies (New York: W. W. Norton & Company, 2014).
22. Etzioni, Amitai, and Oren Etzioni. "Should AI Be Regulated?" Issues in Science and Technology 33, no. 4 (Summer 2017).
23. Furman, Jason (2016). "Is This Time Different? The Opportunities and Challenges of AI." Speech at the 2016 AI Now Conference.
24. Future of Life Institute, "Autonomous Weapons: An Open Letter from AI & Robotics Researchers" (28 July 2015).
25. Galasso, A, and H Luo (2018), "Punishing Robots: Issues in the Economics of Tort Liability and Innovation in AI", in A Agrawal, J
26. Gans, and A Goldfarb (eds), The Economics of AI: An Agenda, University of Chicago Press.
27. Ghahramani, Z. Bayesian non-parametric and the probabilistic approach to modelling. Phil. Trans. R. Soc. A 371, 20110553 (2013). A review of Bayesian non-parametric modelling written for a general scientific audience.
28. Girolami, M. & Calderhead, B. Riemann manifold Langevin and Hamiltonian Monte Carlo methods. J. R. Stat. Soc. Series B Stat. Methodol. 73, 123–214 (2011).
29. Goodman, N. D. & Stuhlmüller, A. The Design and Implementation of Probabilistic Programming Languages. (2015).
30. Goodman, N. D. et al. Relevant and robust a response to Marcus and Davis (2013). Psychol. Sci. 26, 539–541 (2015).
31. Griffiths, T. L. & Tenenbaum, J. B. Optimal predictions in everyday cognition. Psychol. Sci. 17, 767–773 (2006).

32. Goldfarb, A, and C Tucker (2012), "Privacy and Innovation", in J Lerner and S Stern (eds), Innovation Policy and the Economy, Volume 12, NBER, University of Chicago Press: 65-89.
33. Hinton, G. et al. Deep neural networks for acoustic modeling in speech recognition: the shared views of four research groups. IEEE Signal Process. Mag. 29, 82–97 (2012).
34. Hjort, N., Holmes, C., Müller, P. & Walker, S. (eds). Bayesian Nonparametrics (Cambridge Univ. Press, 2010).
35. IEEE, "Ethically Aligned Design" (13 Dec. 2016).
36. Jaynes, E. T. Probability Theory: the Logic of Science (Cambridge Univ. Press, 2003).
37. John Markoff, Machines of Loving Grace: The Quest for Common Ground Between Humans and Robots (New York, NY: ECCO, 2015).
38. Jordan, M., Ghahramani, Z., Jaakkola, T. & Saul, L. An introduction to variational methods in graphical models. Mach. Learn. 37, 183–233 (1999).
39. Kemp, C., Tenenbaum, J. B., Griffiths, T. L., Yamada, T. & Ueda, N. Learning systems of concepts with an infinite relational model. In Proc. 21st National Conference on Artificial Intelligence 381–388 (2006).
40. King, Paul John, Michael Julian Richardson, and Daniel Watts. "Adaptive cruise control system." U.S. Patent No. 6,116,369. 12 Sep. 2000.
41. Knill, D. & Richards, W. Perception as Bayesian inference (Cambridge Univ. Press, 1996).
42. Koller, D. & Friedman, N. Probabilistic Graphical Models: Principles and Techniques (MIT Press, 2009).

43. Krizhevsky, A., Sutskever, I. & Hinton, G. E. ImageNet classification with deep convolutional neural networks. In Proc. Advances in Neural Information Processing Systems 25 1097–1105 (2012).
44. Li, Deyi, and Yi Du. AI with uncertainty. Chapman and Hall/CRC, 2007.
45. Lin, P. et al. eds. 2011. Robot Ethics: The Ethical and Social Implications of Robotics.Cambridge: The MIT Press.
46. Marcus, G. F. & Davis, E. How robust are probabilistic models of higher-level cognition? Psychol. Sci. 24, 2351–2360 (2013).
47. Malli, Nisa, Melinda Jacobs, and Sarah Villeneuve (2018). "Intro to AI for Policymakers: Understanding the shift." Brookfield Institute for Innovation + Entrepreneurship.
48. Neal, R. M. In Handbook of Markov Chain Monte Carlo (eds Brooks, S., Gelman, A., Jones, G. & Meng, X.-L.) (Chapman & Hall/CRC, 2010).
49. Neal, R. M. in Maximum Entropy and Bayesian Methods 197–211 (Springer, 1992).
50. Negnevitsky, Michael. AI: a guide to intelligent systems. Pearson Education, 2005.
51. Orbanz, P. & Teh, Y. W. in Encyclopedia of Machine Learning 81–89 (Springer, 2010).
52. Oren Etzioni, "No, the Experts Don't Think Superintelligent AI is a Threat to Humanity," MIT Technology Review (20 Sept. 2016).
53. Parry, V. et al. 2013. "Principles of Robotics: regulating robots in the real world," Engineering and Physical Sciences. Research Council (EPSRC),

54. Russell, S. & Norvig, P. Artificial Intelligence: a Modern Approach (Prentice–Hall, 1995).
55. Reddy, Raj. "Foundations and grand challenges of AI: AAAI presidential address." AI Magazine 9.4 (1988): 9.
56. Sermanet, P. et al. Over feat: integrated recognition, localization, and detection using convolutional networks. In Proc. International Conference on Learning Representations
57. Stevenson, B (2018), "AI, Income, Employment, and Meaning", in A Agrawal, J Gans, and A Goldfarb (eds), The Economics of AI: An Agenda, University of Chicago Press.
58. Sutskever, I., Vinyals, O. & Le, Q. V. Sequence to sequence learning with neural networks. In Proc. Advances in Neural Information Processing Systems 27, 3104–3112 (2014).
59. Sutton, T (2018), "An Overview of AI Strategies", Medium, 28 June.
60. Tenenbaum, J. B., Kemp, C., Griffiths, T. L. & Goodman, N. D. How to grow a mind: statistics, structure, and abstraction. Science 331, 1279–1285 (2011).
61. Thrun, S., Burgard, W. & Fox, D. Probabilistic Robotics (MIT Press, 2006).
62. Van Horn, K. S. Constructing a logic of plausible inference: a guide to Cox's theorem. Int. J. Approx. Reason.
63. Wolpert, D. M., Ghahramani, Z. & Jordan, M. I. An internal model for sensorimotor integration. Science 269, 1880–1882 (1995).
64. Walker Smith, B. 2016. "How Governments Can Promote Automated Driving,"

65. Yudkowsky, Eliezer (2008). "AI as a Positive and Negative Factor in Global Risk" In Bostrom, Nick and Cirkovic, Milan M. (eds.), Global Catastrophic Risks, pp. 308-345 (Oxford: Oxford University Press).
66. Yudkowsky, Eliezer. "AI as a positive and negative factor in global risk." Global catastrophic risks 1.303 (2008): 184.
67. Freer, C., Roy, D. & Tenenbaum, J. B. in Turing's Legacy (ed. Downey, R.) 195–252 (2014).
68. Marjoram, P., Molitor, J., Plagnol, V. & Tavaré, S. Markov chain Monte Carlo without likelihoods. Proc. Natl Acad. Sci. USA 100, 15324–15328 (2003).
69. Stan Development Team. Stan Modeling Language Users Guide and Reference Manual, Version 2.5.0. (2014).
70. Fischer, B. & Schumann, J. AutoBayes: a system for generating data analysis programs from statistical models. J. Funct. Program. 13, 483–508 (2003).
71. Wingate, D., Stuhlmüller, A. & Goodman, N. D. Lightweight implementations of probabilistic programming languages via transformational compilation. In Proc. International Conference on Artificial Intelligence and Statistics 770–778 (2011).
72. Wood, F., van de Meent, J. W. & Mansinghka, V. A new approach to probabilistic programming inference. In Proc. 17th International Conference on Artificial Intelligence and Statistics 1024–1032 (2014).
73. Jones, D. R., Schonlau, M. & Welch, W. J. Efficient global optimization of expensive black-box functions. J. Glob. Optim. 13, 455–492 (1998).

74. Hennig, P. & Schuler, C. J. Entropy search for information-efficient global optimization. J. Mach. Learn. Res. 13, 1809–1837 (2012).
75. Hernández-Lobato, J. M., Hoffman, M. W. & Ghahramani, Z. Predictive entropy search for efficient global optimization of black-box functions. In Proc. Advances in Neural Information Processing Systems 918–926 (2014).
76. Poupart, P. in Encyclopedia of Machine Learning 90–93 (Springer, 2010).
77. Diaconis, P. in Statistical Decision Theory and Related Topics IV 163–175 (Springer, 1988).

www.ingramcontent.com/pod-product-compliance
Lightning Source LLC
Chambersburg PA
CBHW032211220526
45472CB00018B/829